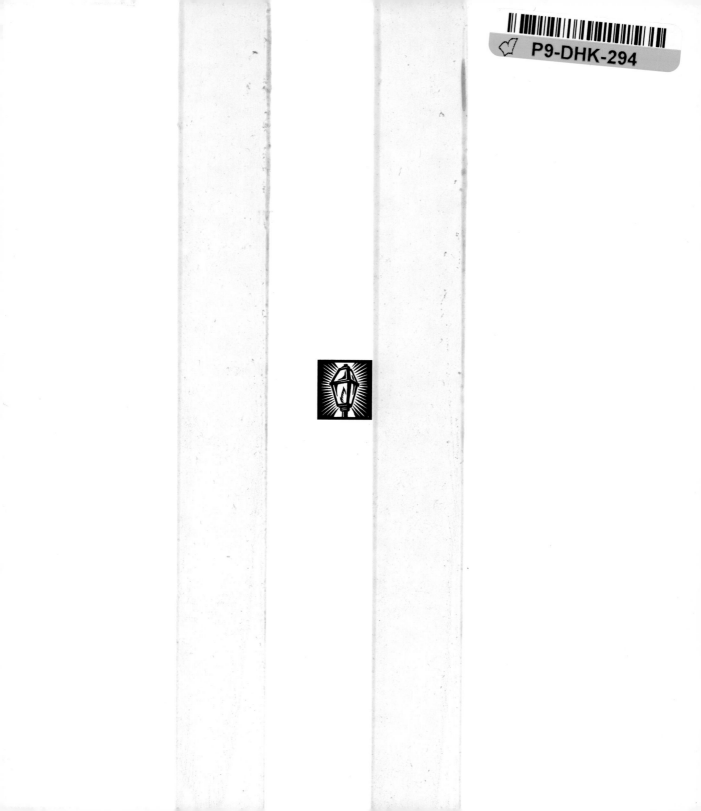

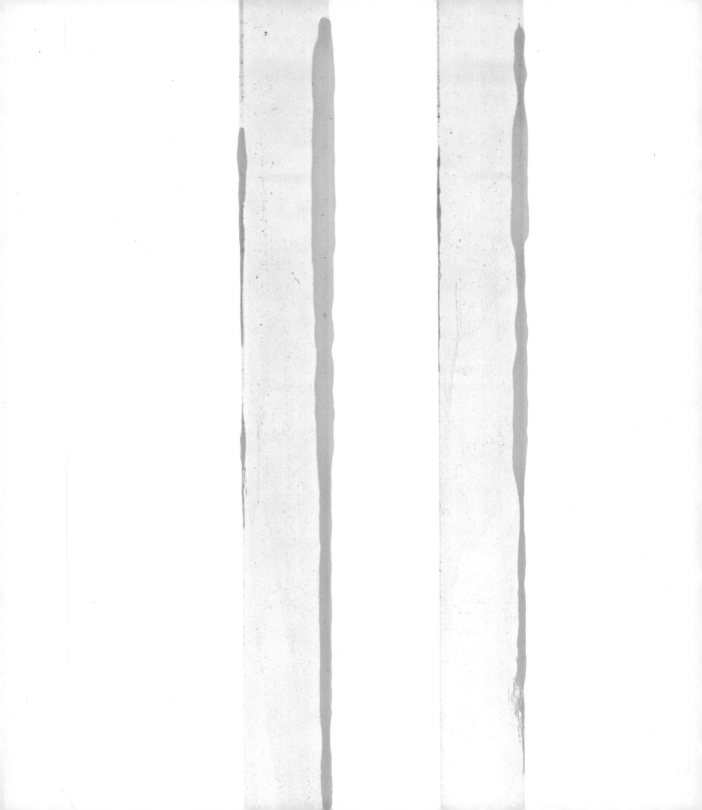

365 QUICK TIPS

365 Quick Tips

Kitchen Tricks and Shortcuts to Make You a
Faster, Smarter, Better Cook

By the Editors of

COOK'S ILLUSTRATED

Illustrations by John Burgoyne and Alan Witschonke

BOSTON COMMON PRESS
Brookline, Massachusetts

Boston Common Press
17 Station Street
Brookline, Massachusetts 02445

ISBN 0-936184-50-7
Library of Congress Cataloging-in-Publication Data
The Editors of Cook's Illustrated
365 Quick Tips: Kitchen tricks and shortcuts to make you a faster, smarter, better cook.
1st Edition

ISBN 0-936184-50-7 $14.95
I. Cooking. I. Title
2000

Manufactured in the United States of America

Distributed by Boston Common Press, 17 Station Street, Brookline, MA 02445.

Designed by Amy Klee
Edited by Jack Bishop
Illustrated by John Burgoyne and Alan Witschonke

Acknowledgments

This book contains the most useful quick tips that have appeared in the pages of *Cook's Illustrated* since the charter issue was published in 1993. Many of the ideas illustrated in this book began as suggestions from readers. We are continually surprised by the ingenuity and common sense expressed in your letters, faxes, and e-mails.

For the past five years, Adam Ried has been the person at the magazine who reads all of this correspondence and figures out which tips are unique enough to publish. He also writes the descriptive captions that bring the drawings to life.

John Willoughby has edited the magazine since its inception and his intelligence comes through in every quick tip.

The test kitchen staff tests the tips and adds their own refinements. Thanks to the efforts of Pam Anderson, Julia Collin, Eva Katz, Bridget Lancaster, Susan Logozzo, Kay Rentschler, Anne Yamanaka, and Dawn Yanagihara, you can be assured that these tips really work.

Jack Bishop combed through the thousands of drawings published in the magazine during the past eight years and turned the best tips into a coherent book. Our talented art director, Amy Klee, designed a book that is easy to use. This project would not exist without the drawings of two illustrators, John Burgoyne and Alan Witschonke. Over the years, their graceful, clear, and informative illustrations have told stories no words ever could.

The art, editorial, and production staffs worked long hours to produce this book. Special thanks to Barbara Bourassa, Rich Cassidy, Mary Connelly, Sheila Datz, Daniel Frey, India Koopman, Jessica Lindheimer, Jim McCormack, Nicole Morris, Nate Nickerson, and Marcia Palmater.

Thanks also to Angela Miller of The Miller Agency.

Contents

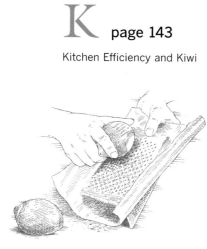

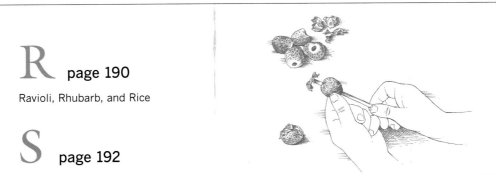

R page 190

Ravioli, Rhubarb, and Rice

S page 192

Saffron, Salad Spinners, Salmon, Salt, Scallions, Scallops, Shallots, Shortening, Shrimp, Soufflés, Soups, Spaghetti, Spices, Squash, Steaming, Stews, Stir-Frying, Stocks, Strawberries, and Stuffing

T page 212

Tartlets, Tarts, Tea, Tomato Paste, Tomatoes, Tongs, Tortillas, Turkey, and Twine

V page 224

V-Rack, Vanilla, and Vegetable Peeler

W page 227

Walnuts and Wine Glasses

Z page 228

Zucchini

Introduction

What is a quick tip? For the editors of *Cook's Illustrated,* it's an easier way of performing a kitchen task which either saves time or money or improves the quality of the outcome. The tip may call for an odd appliance such as a hair dryer (for smoothing chocolate frosting), a surprising ingredient such as miniature marshmallows (placed on the ends of toothpicks to hold plastic wrap above a frosted cake), or a common kitchen tool such as an egg slicer which is used to slice mushrooms.

These tips are the best picks from thousands of techniques and shortcuts submitted by our readers over the last eight years. You will find practical tricks for peeling tomatoes, mincing garlic, and organizing your pantry along with truly original ideas for getting the lumps out of polenta (use an immersion blender), knowing when your steamer is out of water (add marbles to the bottom of the pot), and toasting pine nuts without burning them (use a popcorn popper). You will also find two of my favorite tips: use a coffee maker to melt chocolate and store natural peanut butter upside down so the oil doesn't separate and float to the top.

If you like this book, please join us at *Cook's Illustrated* by contacting us at www.cooksillustrated.com. Submit one of your quick tips, subscribe to the magazine, or ask a question on our bulletin board. Maybe we'll publish one of your kitchen tips in the second edition! All the best.

Christopher Kimball
Editor and Publisher
Cook's Illustrated

QUICK TIPS:
A to Z

Number 1

Anchovies | MINCING

Anchovies often stick to the side of a chef's knife, making it hard to cut them into small bits. Here are two better ways to mince anchovies.

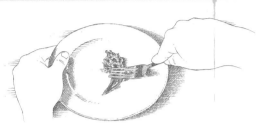

A. Use a dinner fork to mash delicate anchovy fillets into a paste. Mash the fillets on a small plate to catch any oil the anchovies give off.

B. A garlic press will turn anchovies into a fine puree. This method is especially handy when you have already dirtied the press with garlic.

Number 2

Apples | BAKING

Many apples lose their shape when baked. Among common varieties, we find that Golden Delicious apples bake up best. Other good choices include Baldwin, Cortland, Ida Red, and Northern Spy.

1. To allow steam to escape and to keep the apples from bursting in the oven, remove a strip of skin around the apple's stem with a vegetable peeler. Leave the rest of the skin on the apple. We find that the skin helps the apple retain its shape in the oven.

2. Removing the inedible core gives you a chance to stuff a baked apple with brown sugar, nuts, or raisins. The easiest way to core a whole apple is with a melon baller. Just be careful not to puncture the blossom end or the filling may leak out from the bottom of the apple.

Number 3

Apples | CORING

In many recipes, apples are peeled, cored, and then cut into wedges or slices. Start by removing the peel with a paring knife or a vegetable peeler. Next, cut the apple in quarters through the stem end.

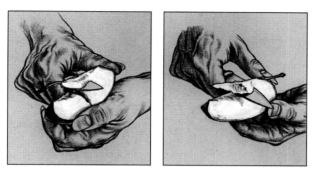

1. A piece of the core can now be removed from each quarter. However, the direction you cut is important. We find that when we start at the stem end, the quarters often break.

2. This problem does not occur if you core the quarters starting at the blossom end. The cored quarter can now be sliced as desired.

Number 4

Artichokes | STEAMING

Whole, trimmed artichokes must remain upright when steamed so that the leaves on one side don't cook faster than the leaves on the other side. When artichokes are stuffed, it is imperative that they don't tip over. Here's an easy way to steady artichokes as they steam.

Cut very thick slices (about 1½ inches) from medium onions and use your fingers to pop the outer three or four rings from the rest of the slice. Set the onion rings on the bottom of the pan and place one artichoke on each ring. In addition to steadying the artichoke, the onion lifts the stem end up from the bottom of the pot and keeps it from overcooking. You can use the band from a canning jar lid in the same fashion.

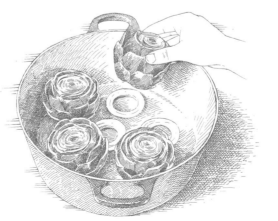

19

Number 5

Asparagus | TRIMMING THE TOUGH ENDS

The tough, woody part of the stem will break off in just the right place—without cutting—if you hold the spear the right way.

With one hand, hold the asparagus about halfway down the stalk; with the thumb and index finger of the other hand, hold the spear about an inch up from the bottom. Bend the stalk until it snaps.

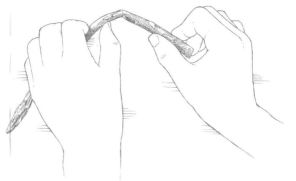

Number 6

Asparagus | ROLL-CUTTING

For stir-frying and pasta sauces, it's best to use small pieces of asparagus that have been cut on the diagonal.

With the knife blade at a 30-degree angle to the asparagus, cut a small piece off the bottom of the spear. Roll the spear one-quarter turn and cut again, maintaining the 30-degree angle between the knife and the asparagus. Repeat the process, rolling the spear a bit after each cut.

Number 7

Avocados |
TESTING FOR RIPENESS

When shopping for avocados, choose the variety with dark, pebbly skin. We find that Haas avocados are creamier and more flavorful than large, smooth-skinned varieties. Squeeze the avocado to judge ripeness. The flesh should yield to moderate pressure.

A soft avocado is sometimes bruised rather than truly ripe. To be sure, try to flick the small stem off the avocado. If it comes off easily and you can see green underneath it, the avocado is ripe and ready to eat. If the stem does not come off or if you see brown underneath after prying it off, the avocado is not ripe.

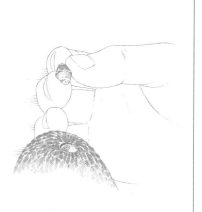

Number 8

Avocados | PITTING

Digging the pit out with a spoon can mar the flesh and is generally a messy proposition. This method solves the problem.

1. Start by slicing around the pit and through both ends with a chef's knife.

2. With your hands, twist to separate the avocado into two halves. Stick the blade of the chef's knife sharply into the pit. Lift the knife, twisting the blade if necessary to loosen and remove the pit.

3. Don't pull the pit off the knife with your hands. Instead, use a large wooden spoon to pry the pit safely off the knife.

Avocados | PEELING AND SLICING

Once an avocado has been pitted, you may want to remove neat slices, especially for salads.

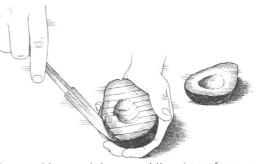

1. Use a paring knife to slice through the meat, but not the skin.

2. Run a rubber spatula around the circumference, just inside the skin, to loosen the avocado flesh. Once the flesh has been loosened from the skin, twist the spatula to pop out the meat.

Bacon | STORING

Now that many people eat bacon less often and in smaller amounts, it can be difficult to use up a pound, once opened, before it becomes rancid. Freezing is the best way to preserve bacon, but if frozen in the original package, it's impossible to remove just a few slices as needed later.

To solve this dilemma, roll up the bacon in tight cylinders, each with two to four slices of bacon. Place the cylinders in a zipper-lock plastic bag and place the bag flat in the freezer. (Once the slices are frozen, the bag can be stored as you like.) When bacon is needed, simply pull out the desired number of slices and defrost.

Number 11

Bacon Drippings | SAVING FOR ANOTHER USE

Bacon grease is a prized flavor in many dishes, especially from the South. Instead of keeping a bulky jar in the refrigerator, we like to store bacon drippings in the freezer.

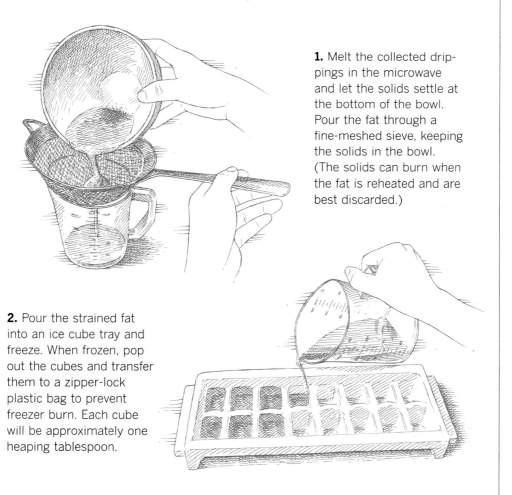

1. Melt the collected drippings in the microwave and let the solids settle at the bottom of the bowl. Pour the fat through a fine-meshed sieve, keeping the solids in the bowl. (The solids can burn when the fat is reheated and are best discarded.)

2. Pour the strained fat into an ice cube tray and freeze. When frozen, pop out the cubes and transfer them to a zipper-lock plastic bag to prevent freezer burn. Each cube will be approximately one heaping tablespoon.

Number 12

Bagels | SHAPING A STIFF DOUGH INTO RINGS

It can be difficult to shape stiff doughs, especially for bagels, into rings. Rather than trying to roll the dough into ropes and attach the ends (which may not stick together), try this method.

1. Slightly flatten each ball of dough with the palm of your hand.

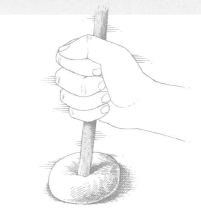

2. Punch through the center of the ball with the handle of a wooden spoon.

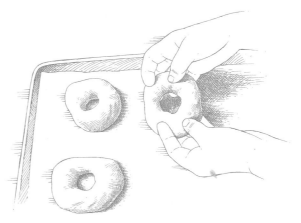

3. Holding the spoon by the handle, spin it gently to enlarge the dough ring to the desired size.

4. Stretch the hole with your fingers as you place the dough ring on a baking sheet.

Number 13

Baking | KEEPING TRACK OF DRY INGREDIENTS

When a recipe calls for a number of dry ingredients to be added simultaneously (such as baking powder, baking soda, salt, and spices), it's easy to lose track of what's been added to the bowl, especially if you get interrupted.

We prefer to place the measured ingredients in separate mounds on a sheet of parchment or waxed paper. This way you can see not only what but also how much you have measured.

Number 14

Baking | MEASURING LIQUIDS

Because holding a cup will jostle or tilt the liquid, it can destroy the accuracy of the measurements that might make all the difference when baking.

To avoid possible mismeasurements, pour liquids into clear measuring cups set on the counter and lean down to read them at eye level.

Number 15

Baking Powder | TESTING FOR FRESHNESS

Baking powder will lose its leavening ability with time. We suggest writing the date the can was opened on a piece of tape and affixing the tape to the bottom of the can. After six months, baking powder will begin to weaken and after a year it should be discarded. If you have any doubts about the strength of your baking powder, use this test.

Mix 2 teaspoons of baking powder with one cup of hot tap water. If there's an immediate reaction of fizzing and foaming (right), the baking powder can be used. If the reaction is at all delayed or weak (left), throw the baking powder away and buy a fresh can.

Number 16

Bananas | SAVING OVERRIPE FRUIT FOR BREAD

Rather than throwing away one or two overripe bananas, they can be saved until you have enough fruit to make banana bread.

Place overripe bananas in a zipper-lock plastic bag and freeze. As needed, add more bananas to the bag. When you are ready to make bread, thaw the bananas on the counter until softened.

Number 17

Bar Cookies | FROSTING WITH CHOCOLATE

Here's an easy way to give blondies, brownies, and other bar cookies a chocolate topping without having to use a double boiler or the microwave to melt the chocolate.

1. When the pan comes out of the oven, lay a large chocolate bar, broken into several pieces, directly on top of the hot bar cookies.

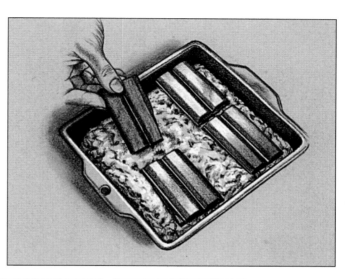

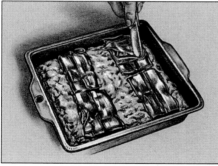

2. Once the chocolate bar has softened and begun to melt, use a table knife to spread it out.

3. Continue spreading until the chocolate makes a thin, even layer over the entire top. Cool the bar cookies completely to allow the chocolate frosting to firm up.

Number 18

Barbecue Sauce | APPLYING WITH A SQUEEZE BOTTLE

Instead of brushing barbecue sauce onto foods (and dirtying both the brush and bowl), recycle a pull-top spring water bottle by filling it with sauce and keeping it in the refrigerator until needed.

During the last minutes of grilling (when the chicken, pork chops, or other food is almost done), squirt a little sauce onto the food, taking care not to let the bottle touch the food. Wipe the bottle clean and store it in the refrigerator until the next time you grill.

Number 19

Basil | BRUISING LEAVES TO RELEASE FLAVORFUL OILS

The slow grinding action of a mortar and pestle crushes basil leaves and releases their flavorful oils. It's easy to make pesto in a food processor or blender, but the fast grinding action of the blades doesn't create the richest tasting sauce. For the fullest flavor in pesto and other sauces, we find it best to bruise basil leaves before placing them in a food processor or blender. This trick also works with other soft herbs, especially mint and cilantro.

Place the basil leaves in a zipper-lock plastic bag and bruise with a meat pounder or rolling pin.

Number 20

Bean Sprouts | KEEPING THEM CRISP AND FRESH

Bean sprouts are prized for their crunch, not their flavor. To keep them crisp, try this tip, which also works with peeled jicama slices.

Submerge the sprouts in a container of cold water, then refrigerate the container. The sprouts will stay crisp for up to five days.

Number 21

Beef: *Kebabs* | BUTTERFLYING THE MEAT

Marinades can flavor only the exterior of the beef chunks destined for skewering on kebabs. However, if you cut the meat into really small chunks (and thus increase the surface area), the meat tends to overcook before the exterior is nicely browned. Cutting the meat as follows increases the surface area exposed to the marinade and makes more flavorful kebabs. Best of all, the cooking time of the meat is the same. When it's time to grill the meat, simply thread pieces onto the skewers as if they were still cubes.

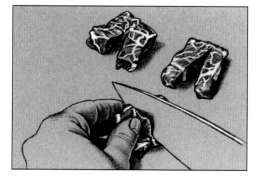

Cut the meat into large cubes. Cut each cube almost through at the center, making sure to leave the meat attached at one end. The meat is ready to be marinated.

2 9

Number 22

Beef: *Prime Rib* | TYING UP A ROAST

In the oven, the outer layer of meat often pulls away from the rib-eye muscle and overcooks.

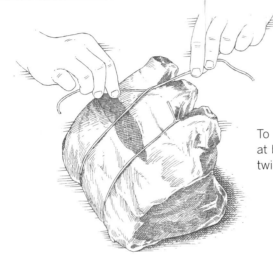

To prevent this problem, tie the roast at both ends, running the kitchen twine parallel to the bone.

Number 23

Beef: *Steak* | CHECKING THE INTERNAL TEMPERATURE

Most instant-read thermometers work best when the tip is stuck at least an inch deep into foods. On a thin steak, the tip can go right through the meat if inserted from the top. Use this tip for steaks as well as chops.

For the most accurate reading, hold the steak with a pair of tongs and slide the tip of the thermometer through the side of the steak. Make sure that the shaft is embedded in the meat and not touching any bone. The steaks are done when the temperature registers 120 degrees for rare, 125 to 130 degrees for medium-rare, and 135 to 140 degrees for medium.

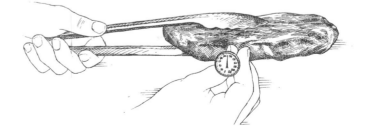

Number 24

Beef: *Steak* | GRILLING T-BONE STEAKS EVENLY

T-bone and porterhouse steaks contain portions of the delicate, buttery tenderloin as well as some of the chewier, more flavorful strip. With their two cuts of meat, these steaks are especially enjoyable to eat but somewhat challenging to cook. A two-level fire (see tip 199, page 132), with more coals banked to one side than the other, helps even out the rate at which these two muscles cook.

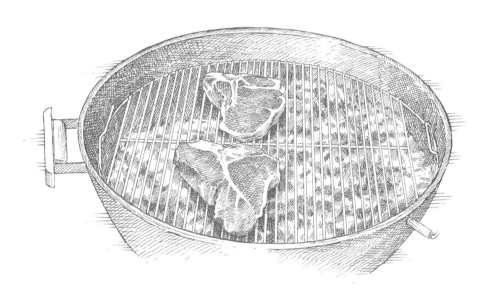

When grilling T-bone and porterhouse steaks, keep the tenderloin (the smaller portion on the left side of the bone) over the cooler part of the fire. The strip (the larger portion on the right side of the bone) should be placed over the hottest part of the fire.

Number 25

Beef: *Steak* | SLICING T-BONE STEAKS

A thick T-bone or porterhouse steak weighs between 1½ and 2 pounds, too much for a single serving. Here's how to serve one steak to two people. Once cooked, let the steak rest for five minutes so the juices can redistribute themselves evenly throughout the meat.

1. Start by slicing close to the bone to remove the larger strip section.

2. Turn the steak around and cut the smaller tenderloin section off the bone.

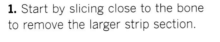

3. Slice each piece crosswise into ⅓-inch-thick portions. Make sure each person gets some tenderloin as well as some strip meat.

Number 26

Beef: *Stir-Fries* | SLICING FLANK STEAK THINLY

Flank steak is our favorite cut for stir-fries. It has the right balance of tenderness (with some chew) and beef flavor. It must be sliced as thinly as possible and a sharp knife is essential. Freezing the meat for 30 to 60 minutes also helps.

1. Slice the partially frozen flank steak into 2-inch-wide pieces.

2. Cut each piece of flank steak against the grain into very thin slices.

Number 27

Beef: *Tenderloin* | CUTTING THE SILVER SKIN

The tenderloin is covered with a thin, shiny membrane called the silver skin. In the oven, the silver skin will contract and can cause the roast to bow. Rather than trying to peel off this very thin membrane, use this technique to keep it from bowing the meat. The same technique can be used with a pork tenderloin.

Slide a knife under the silver skin and flick the blade upward to cut through the membrane. Do this at five or six spots along the length of the roast.

Number 28

Beef: *Tenderloin* | TYING TO ENSURE EVEN COOKING

The tenderloin narrows at one end, called the tip. If roasted or grilled as is, this end will be overcooked by the time the thicker end is done.

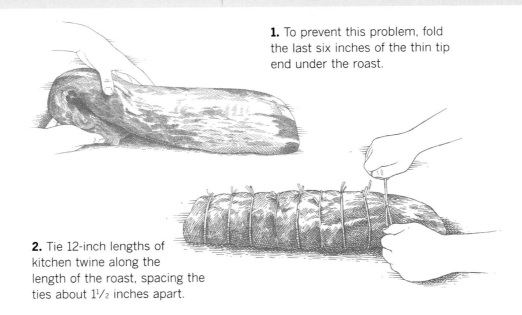

1. To prevent this problem, fold the last six inches of the thin tip end under the roast.

2. Tie 12-inch lengths of kitchen twine along the length of the roast, spacing the ties about 1$^1/_2$ inches apart.

Number 29

Beets |
REMOVING STAINS

When cut, beets stain everything they touch, including hands and cutting boards.

To help remove these stains, sprinkle the stained area with salt, rinse, and then scrub with soap. The salt crystals help lift the beet juices away.

Number 30

Biscotti | QUICK-DRYING ON A RACK

Traditionally, biscotti dough is baked in a log, then cut into slices and baked a second time. These slices must be flipped halfway through the baking time to dry both sides of each slice. Here's how to streamline this method.

Bake the dough in a log as usual and then cut into slices. Place the slices on a wire cooling rack set on a cookie sheet and bake again. The rack elevates the slices, allowing air to circulate all around them and drying both sides at once.

Number 31

Biscuits | CUTTING WITH A BENCH SCRAPER

If you don't own a biscuit cutter, try this method for shaping and cutting biscuit dough. You can shape and cut scones the same way.

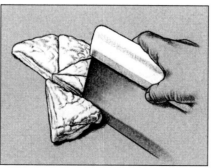

1. Press the dough evenly into an 8-inch cake pan. Flip the circle of dough onto a lightly floured work surface.

2. Using a bench scraper or chef's knife, cut the dough into wedges. Transfer the wedges to a parchment-lined baking sheet and bake.

Number 32

Biscuits | SPLITTING FOR SHORTCAKES

It's important to split biscuits evenly when making shortcakes. A knife sometimes tears the biscuits and isn't necessarily the best tool for the job.

When the biscuits have cooled slightly, look for a crack that naturally forms around the circumference of each biscuit. Gently insert your fingers into the crack and split the biscuit in half.

Number 33

Blanching | SHOCKING VEGETABLES IN A STRAINER

Vegetables, especially green ones, are often partially cooked in boiling water (a process called blanching) to set their color. To prevent them from becoming mushy, blanched vegetables are often "shocked" in ice water to stop the cooking process.

Drain the vegetables into a strainer, and plunge the strainer into a bowl of ice water. With this method, there's no fishing around for vegetables once they have cooled down. Simply lift the strainer from the ice water and let the water drain back into the bowl.

Number 34

Blender | QUICK CLEANING

Washing the blender jar can be a real chore, especially if foods have had time to harden. Get a head start on the cleaning process by following this method.

1. Fill the dirty blender halfway with hot water and add a couple of drops of liquid dish soap.

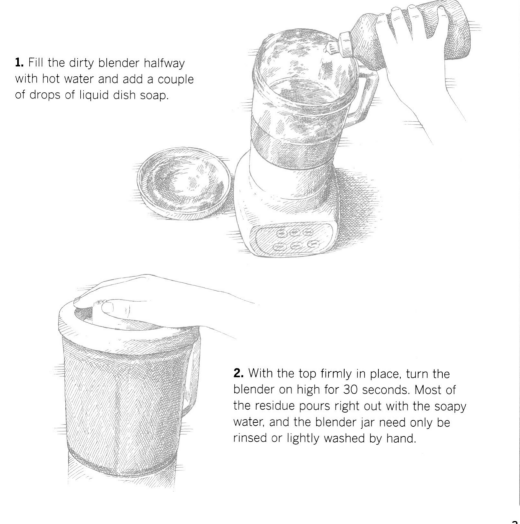

2. With the top firmly in place, turn the blender on high for 30 seconds. Most of the residue pours right out with the soapy water, and the blender jar need only be rinsed or lightly washed by hand.

Number 35

Bok Choy | SLICING WHITES AND GREENS

The thick, fleshy white stalks take much longer to cook than the tender, leafy greens. For this reason, you must slice them separately, so the whites can be added to a stir-fry or other dish first.

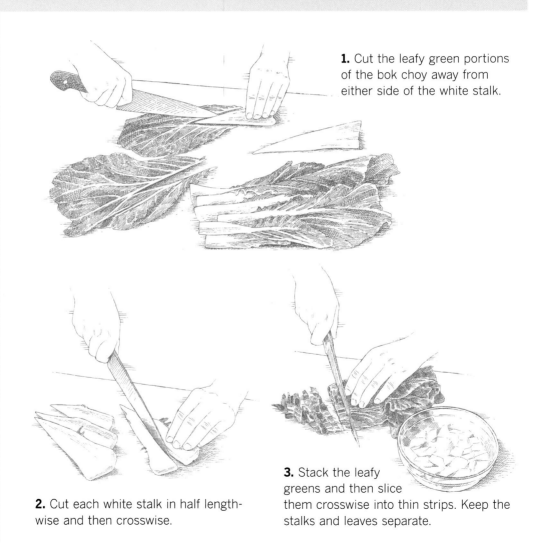

1. Cut the leafy green portions of the bok choy away from either side of the white stalk.

2. Cut each white stalk in half lengthwise and then crosswise.

3. Stack the leafy greens and then slice them crosswise into thin strips. Keep the stalks and leaves separate.

Number 36

Bread | PERFECT SLICES FROM CRUSTY LOAVES

With their heavy crusts, artisan breads can pose a challenge when it comes to slicing neatly. Often, the bread knife fails to cut all the way through the thick bottom crust. The result is that you must yank the slice free from the loaf, often tearing it in the process. Here's how to slice a crusty loaf neatly.

Turn the loaf on its side so that you are cutting through the top and bottom crust simultaneously. The crust on the side of the bread, which is now facing down, is usually much thinner and easier to slice.

Number 37

Bread | FRESHENING STALE LOAVES AND SLICES

We all know bread goes stale very quickly. Here are two tricks for reviving slightly stale loaves and slices. Neither trick will work with rock-hard, days-old bread.

A. Place a stale loaf of bread inside a brown paper bag, seal the bag, and lightly moisten the outside of the bag with some water. Place the bag on a baking sheet in a 350-degree oven for five minutes. When you remove the loaf, you will find it is warm and soft.

B. Individual slices of stale bread can be freshened on a splatter screen held over a pan of simmering water. The rising steam will soften the bread in a minute or two.

Number 38

Bread: *Making the Dough* | CLEANING UP THE BOWL

Cleaning dough from a bowl or work surface can be difficult. Soapy water and a sponge simply can't get the job done, and soaking the bowl doesn't really help. A steel wool scrubbing pad is the most effective tool for lifting dough from surfaces, but the pad is good for little else once it has been used this way. To save money, try this tip.

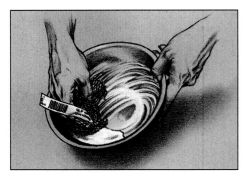

Save the plastic mesh bags used to package shallots, onions, and potatoes for lifting away sticking dough from bowls and other surfaces. Once the dough is attached to the mesh bag, throw it away and then wash out the bowl with soapy water.

Number 39

Bread: *Making the Dough* | JUDGING WHEN BREAD HAS ENOUGH FLOUR

Most bakers add too much flour to bread dough, which can result in dry loaves. Here's an easy test to see if your bread has enough flour.

Squeeze the dough gently with your entire hand. Even with especially soft, sticky doughs, your hand will pull away cleanly once the dough has enough flour.

Number 40

Bread: *Rising and Shaping* | COVERING THE DOUGH

Once the dough is ready to rise, most recipes suggest putting it into a deep bowl and covering the bowl with a damp kitchen towel. We find that the towel won't stop drafts from attacking the dough.

Instead, tightly seal the bowl with plastic wrap, which keeps out drafts and traps moisture so the dough remains supple.

Number 41

Bread: *Rising and Shaping* | MAKESHIFT PROOFING BOX

Bread making can be tricky in a cold, drafty kitchen. Professional bakers let dough rise in large proofing boxes that are warm and free of drafts. This makeshift arrangement works just like a professional proofing box.

Heat a measuring cup filled with a cup of water to the boiling point in a microwave. Turn off the microwave and then place the bowl with the dough inside and close the door. The preheated water keeps the dough at a warm temperature while the microwave keeps drafts at bay.

Number 42

Bread: *Rising and Shaping* | DRAFT-FREE RISING IN A LOAF PAN

Some doughs should rise right in a loaf pan just before baking. (This is called the second rise.) If your kitchen is drafty, the dough may not rise properly. Here's a defense against a drafty environment.

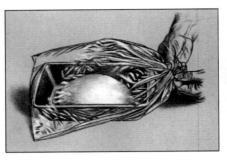 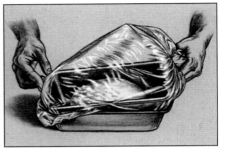

1. After forming the dough and placing it in a loaf pan, slip the pan into an empty plastic bag. Blow air into the bag to inflate it, then seal it securely with a twist tie.

2. Place this loaf pan into another loaf pan so that the air inside the bag is pushed up, providing room for the dough to expand.

Number 43

Bread: *Rising and Shaping* | MEASURING BREAD AND PASTRY DOUGHS

Often recipes instruct you to shape dough into loaves of a specific length. Pastry recipes may instruct you to roll dough to a specific size. Rather than fumbling in drawers with messy hands to find a ruler each time, put this tip to work.

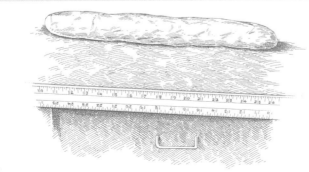

Affix a yardstick to the front of a countertop. It's not obtrusive, and it's always there when you need it. To measure doughs, simply line up the ends with markings on the ruler and do the math.

Number 44

Bread: *Rising and Shaping* | SLASHING WITH SHEARS

Slashes in risen bread dough help it to expand evenly as it bakes. Professionals use a tool called a lamé. A single-edge razor blade can be used, too. If you can't find a razor blade, don't use a knife, which can pull or tear the dough and cause it to deflate. Kitchen shears can slash dough cleanly and easily if you don't have a razor blade.

Open the blades on a sharp pair of kitchen shears. Lower the scissors toward the dough and quickly snip to slash the top of the bread in several places.

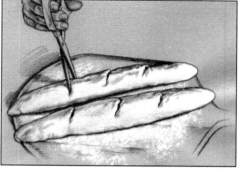

Number 45

Bread: *Baking* | ADDING WATER TO THE OVEN

Placing a pan of boiling water in the oven while bread is baking helps to ensure a crisp crust. It can also cause a nasty scalding. The following method of adding moisture to the oven is safe, and it can also be used for a bain marie (water bath).

Use a copper watering can with a long spout to pour boiling water into a pan that's been preheated in the oven.

Number 46

Bread: *Baking* | TAKING THE TEMPERATURE IN A LOAF PAN

Internal temperature is a good way to gauge whether or not a loaf of bread is done. You may be tempted to pierce the top crust in the center, but that method leaves behind a conspicuous hole.

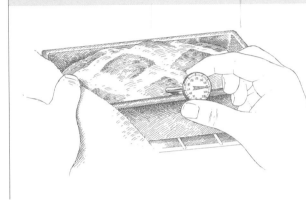

We prefer to insert the thermometer from the side, just above the edge of the loaf pan, directing it at a downward angle toward the center of the loaf.

Number 47

Bread Crumbs | SLICING OFF THE TOUGH BOTTOM CRUST

Homemade bread crumbs are far superior to commercial dry crumbs. To make your own crumbs, simply grind cubes of stale bread in a food processor until coarsely chopped. There's one hitch: Many loaves of bread have an overbaked bottom crust that won't break down in a food processor.

To prevent this problem, simply slice off and discard the bottom crust before cutting the bread into large cubes that will fit in the food processor.

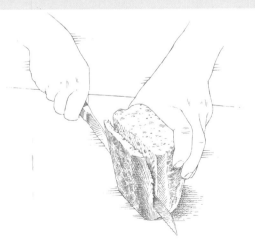

Number 48

Broccoli | TWO WAYS TO REMOVE FLORETS

Some heads of broccoli have closely bunched branches that meet the central stalk at roughly the same point. On other heads, the branches are widely spaced. You should adjust the way you remove florets, depending on how a head of broccoli is shaped.

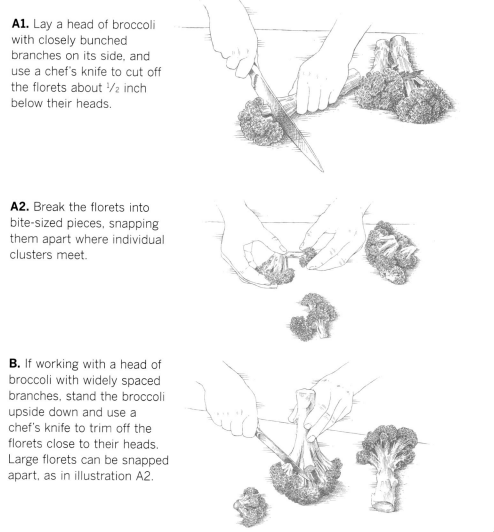

A1. Lay a head of broccoli with closely bunched branches on its side, and use a chef's knife to cut off the florets about $1/2$ inch below their heads.

A2. Break the florets into bite-sized pieces, snapping them apart where individual clusters meet.

B. If working with a head of broccoli with widely spaced branches, stand the broccoli upside down and use a chef's knife to trim off the florets close to their heads. Large florets can be snapped apart, as in illustration A2.

Number 49

Brown Sugar | SOFTENING

There's nothing worse than hardened brown sugar, which is impossible to measure and can't be incorporated into batters. Here's how to bring back its original texture.

Place a cup or so of brown sugar in a glass pie plate or bowl, cover with a small piece of waxed paper, and then top with a slice of bread to provide a bit of moisture. Loosely cover the pie plate or bowl with plastic wrap and microwave until softened, about 30 seconds.

Number 50

Brown Sugar | MEASURING

Recipes usually call for "firmly packed" brown sugar. Here's our tip for getting an accurate measurement without fuss.

Fill the correct dry measure with brown sugar and use the next smallest cup to pack it down. For instance, if you need 1/2 cup firmly packed brown sugar, use the bottom of the 1/3 cup measure to pack it down.

Number 51

Brownies | LINING THE PAN

Brownies, especially fudgy ones, can stick to a baking pan. We line baking pans with foil whenever making brownies or any other bar cookies.

1. Coat the baking pan with nonstick vegetable cooking spray. Fit one sheet of aluminum foil, folded to be slightly narrower than the pan, into the greased pan, pushing it into the corners and up the sides of the pan. Make sure the foil overhangs a bit. Fit a second sheet of foil into the pan in the same manner, placing it perpendicular to the first sheet. If the recipe calls for greasing the pan, spray the foil liberally.

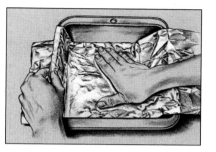

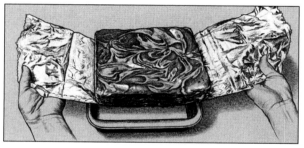

2. Add the batter to the pan, then bake and cool as directed. Use the foil handles to lift the brownies from the pan in a single piece. Cut into bars as directed.

Number 52

Brushes | GETTING THEM CLEAN

It can be very difficult to clean a basting brush that has been dipped in oil or sauce. As a result, the bristles often remain sticky and sometimes even get smelly as the brush sits in a drawer between uses. Here's a better way to care for your brushes.

Wash the dirty brushes thoroughly with liquid dish soap and very hot water, then rinse well and shake dry. Place the brushes, bristles pointing down, into a cup and fill the cup with coarse salt until the bristles are covered. The salt draws moisture out of the bristles and keeps them dry and fresh between uses. The next time you need a brush, simply shake off the salt, and you're ready to go.

Number 53

Burgers | GETTING AN ACCURATE TEMPERATURE READING

It's hard to get an accurate temperature reading even in the thickest burgers. While we like to hold steaks and chops with tongs and slide an instant-read thermometer through the side (see tip 23, page 30), we find this technique can cause delicate burgers to break apart.

Instead, slide the tip of the thermometer into the burger at the top edge and push toward the center.

Number 54

Butter | SHAVING THIN SLICES OVER CASSEROLES

Many recipes for casseroles and pies direct the cook to dot the surface with butter just before putting the dish into the oven. Instead of dicing butter (which is a messy proposition), try this neater method.

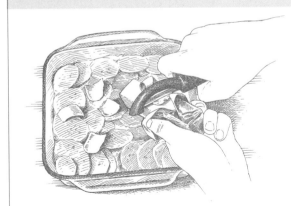

Use a vegetable peeler to shave the desired amount of butter off a frozen stick, letting the pieces fall onto the food in fine curls.

Number 55

Butter | MAKING COMPOUND BUTTERS

Compound butters (softened butter mixed with citrus zest, chopped herbs, minced ginger or garlic, and other seasonings) are a quick way to add rich flavor to grilled or roasted fish, chicken, chops, or steaks. Once the butter has been shaped, it can be frozen for up to three months.

1. Place the compound butter on top of a piece of waxed paper.

2. Roll the butter into a long, narrow cylinder. Transfer the paper-wrapped cylinder to a zipper-lock plastic bag and freeze.

3. When you need it, take the butter out of the freezer, unwrap it, and cut off rounds about 1/2 inch thick. Place the rounds on top of freshly cooked hot foods and let them melt as you carry plates to the table.

Number 56

Butter | GRATING BUTTER INTO FLOUR

Many cooks use their fingertips to cut butter into flour, but we find the heat from your hands can cause the butter to melt. We think the food processor is the best tool for cutting butter into flour to make pie pastry or biscuits. If you don't have a food processor, try this method.

1. Rub a frozen stick of butter against the large holes of a regular box grater over the bowl with the flour.

2. Once all the butter has been grated, use a pastry blender or two table knives to work the butter into the flour. Keep cutting the butter in until the pieces are pea-sized.

Number 57

Butter | KNOWING WHEN BUTTER IS PROPERLY SOFTENED

To cream butter for cookies or cakes, the butter must be brought to cool room temperature (about 67 degrees) so that it is malleable but not soft. Don't hurry this step. Cold butter can't hold as much air as properly softened butter, and the resulting cakes and cookies may be too dense. If you don't have an instant-read thermometer to take the temperature of butter, use these visual clues.

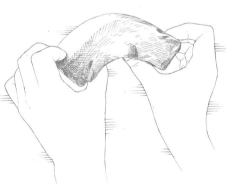

1. When you unwrap the butter, the wrapping should have a creamy residue on the inside. If there's no residue, the butter is probably too cold.

2. The butter should bend with little resistance and without cracking or breaking.

3. The butter should give slightly when pressed but still hold its shape.

Number 58

Butter | SOFTENING BUTTER IN A HURRY

It can take a long time for a stick of chilled butter to reach the right temperature for creaming. Many cooks are tempted to use the microwave, but this is an imperfect solution since the edges of the butter often begin to melt before the center is really softened. If you are in a hurry, cut the butter into tablespoon-sized pieces. We find that it will soften to the right stage in about 15 minutes.

If, despite all precautions, your butter is still too cool, a quick remedy is to wrap the bowl with a warm, damp towel and continue creaming.

Number 59

Cabbage | REMOVING LEAVES ONE AT A TIME

As fans of stuffed cabbage know, removing leaves from a head of cabbage without tearing them is a daunting task, even after parboiling. Here's a way to get the job done neatly, without the bother of precooking the cabbage.

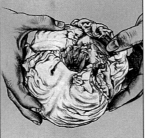
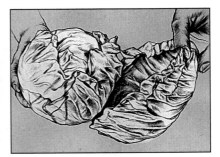

1. Use a sharp paring knife to cut around the core at the base of the cabbage.

2. Remove the core and grasp each individual leaf at its base rather than its outer edge.

3. Gently lift the leaf away from the cabbage. Repeat until you have removed all the large outer leaves you need.

Number 60

Cabbage | CUTTING THROUGH A BIG HEAD

Because most heads of cabbage are at least the size of your chef's knife, it can be hard to figure out how to cut them. We've found the following technique works well.

1. Start by placing the heel of your palm on the back of the knife, a little in front of center, and applying pressure toward the tip of the knife as it goes into the cabbage.

2. Once the blade is completely below the top of the cabbage, move your fingers to the top of the front section of the knife and apply pressure to finish cutting.

Number 61

Cabbage | TWO WAYS TO SHRED

For many recipes, including coleslaw, cabbage should be cut into long, thin strips. This process is called shredding. Start by cutting the cabbage into quarters (see tip 60, page 53).

1. Cut away the hard piece of core attached to each quarter.

2. Separate the cored cabbage quarters into stacks of leaves that flatten when pressed lightly.

3. You have two choices at this point.
A. Use a chef's knife to cut each stack diagonally (this ensures long pieces) into thin shreds.

B. Roll the stacked leaves crosswise to fit them into the feed tube of a food processor fitted with a shredding disk.

Number 62

Cakes | LINING THE PAN AND SERVING PLATTER

Most recipes call for lining cake pans with parchment paper to ensure easy removal. It's also a good idea to line a serving plate with parchment paper before decorating the cake so that excess frosting and nuts do not soil the plate. The strips are then removed once you've finished decorating. Here's how to use one piece of parchment to do both jobs.

1. Trace the bottom of your cake pan roughly in the center of a sheet of parchment paper. (Use a double sheet if making two cake layers.)

2. Fold the traced circle in half and then in half again, then cut just inside the outline of the quarter circle. The resulting round of parchment will fit your pan exactly.

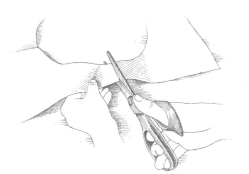 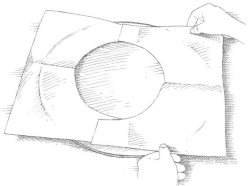

3. Cut the remainder of the sheet in half so that it makes an adjustable circle.

4. This circle will fit perfectly around the cake on the serving plate, keeping the plate rims neat while you frost and decorate.

Number 63

Cakes | DIVIDING THE BATTER

It's important to divide the batter evenly between pans so that the layers are the same height when baked. Eyeballing the batter can be tricky.

To ensure that you put equal amounts of batter in each cake pan, use a kitchen scale to measure the weight of each filled pan.

Number 64

Cakes | FILLING TUBE PANS WITH BATTER

Many bakers know the frustration of spilling batter down the hole in the center of a tube pan. Here's how to keep that batter from running inside the tube, where it can burn and cause a mess.

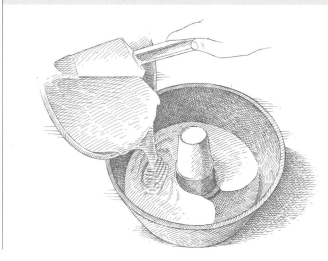

After the pan has been prepared (greased and/or lined with parchment paper), set a small paper cup over the center tube. You can now scrape the batter into the pan without worrying that some may end up in the tube.

Number 65

Cakes | TESTING FOR DONENESS

When testing an especially deep or thick cake, such as a Bundt cake, chiffon cake, or angel food cake, a toothpick won't be long enough and a knife will create too big a hole. Here's how to see if crumbs cling to a tester without marring the surface too much.

Stick an uncooked strand of spaghetti deep into the center of the cake and remove. If the spaghetti is covered with moist batter, the cake needs more time in the oven.

Number 66

Cakes | REMOVING BUNDT CAKE FROM A PAN

Bundt cakes look great, but the ridged interior surface of the pan can be difficult to grease, and the cakes often stick as a result. Here's how to coax the baked cake out of the pan in one piece.

 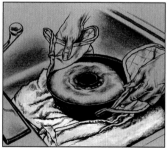 

1. Near the end of baking, place a folded bathroom towel in the sink and saturate it with steaming hot water.

2. When you take the cake out of the oven, immediately set the pan on the towel and leave it there for 10 seconds.

3. Invert the cake onto a cooling rack. It will come out easily and without sticking.

Cakes | ALIGNING THE LAYERS

When you want to make a cake with more than two layers, you will need to split the baked layers in half horizontally. However, if you cut the layers a bit unevenly (which is bound to happen), the cake can lean to one side or the other. Here's a neat trick that helps compensate for less-than-perfect cutting.

1. Place the cooled cake layers on top of each other and make a $\frac{1}{8}$-inch-deep cut down the side of each cake layer with a serrated knife.

2. Split the cake layers, and then begin to fill and assemble the cake, realigning the vertical cuts in the side of each layer. By putting the layers back in their original orientation to each other, you will conceal any unevenness in the way you cut them.

Cakes | TRANSPORTING A FROSTED CAKE

The tried-and-true method for keeping plastic wrap from touching a gooey frosting or glaze is to stick the food with toothpicks and place the wrap over the toothpicks. Occasionally, though, the sharp points of the toothpicks puncture the wrap, which can then slide down and stick to the frosting. To keep the wrap securely above the frosting, try this method.

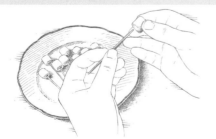

1. Place a miniature marshmallow over the point of each toothpick.

2. Insert toothpicks into cake, with the marshmallows facing up. Lay the plastic wrap over the marshmallows.

Number 69

Cakes | IMPROVISING A COVER

A glass cake plate with a footed stand and large domed cover is the ideal place to store a frosted cake. Here's how to keep a cake fresh and safe from kitchen accidents if you don't own a cake plate.

Turn the outside bowl of a large salad spinner upside down and place it over the frosted cake, resting the bowl on the edge of the cake plate.

Number 70

Cakes: *Frosting* | ANCHORING THE BOTTOM LAYER

Once the cake layers have cooled, it's time to frost them. We find it best to frost a cake on a cardboard round, cut slightly larger than the cake layers. The cardboard supports the cake and makes it easy to move around.

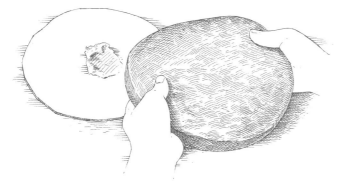

Use a dab of frosting to anchor the cake layer to the cardboard round.

Number 71

Cakes: *Frosting* | KEEPING THE FILLING FROM BLEEDING

Often a raspberry jam filling will bleed through white icing and mar the appearance of the cake. Here's how to keep fillings from seeping through the frosting.

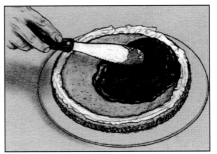

1. Add frosting to a pastry bag fitted with a plain round tip. Pipe a circle of frosting around the top edge of any layer that will be covered with filling— that is, all except the top layer.

2. Spoon some filling into the center of the cake and use a spatula to spread it inside the frosting ring, which will seal the layers of the cake together and prevent the filling from seeping out.

Number 72

Cakes: *Frosting* | GETTING THE TOP LAYER IN PLACE

It can be tricky to lift a top cake layer into place. If you use your hands, the layer may break. Here's a safe way to position the top layer.

Place the layer on a cardboard round or on the removable bottom of a tart pan, and then slide the cake into place.

Number 73

Cakes: *Frosting* | PUTTING A PATTERN IN THE ICING

Once a cake has been frosted, there are several ways to style the icing.

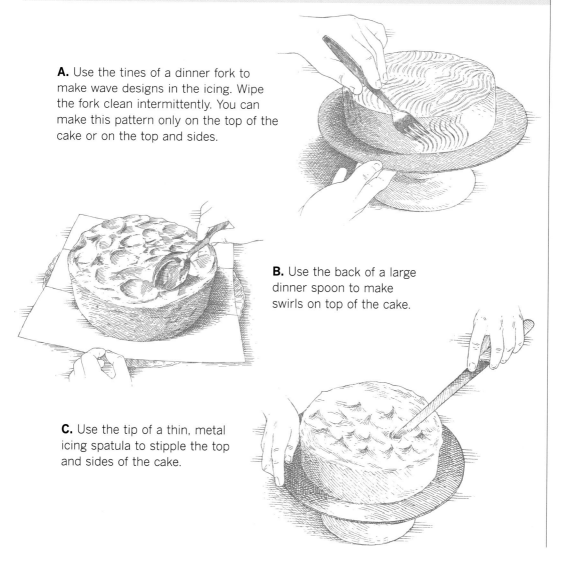

A. Use the tines of a dinner fork to make wave designs in the icing. Wipe the fork clean intermittently. You can make this pattern only on the top of the cake or on the top and sides.

B. Use the back of a large dinner spoon to make swirls on top of the cake.

C. Use the tip of a thin, metal icing spatula to stipple the top and sides of the cake.

Number 74

Cakes: *Frosting|* USING A BLOW DRYER TO CREATE A SILKY LOOK

Professionally decorated cakes seem to have a molten, silky look.

To get that same appearance at home, frost as usual and then use a hair dryer to "blow-dry" the frosted surfaces of the cake. The slight melting of the frosting gives it that smooth, lustrous appearance.

Number 75

Cakes: *Decorating|* FINISHING WITH NUTS

The shape and color of sliced almonds lend themselves to simple, elegant designs. Here are two tips that can be used singly or in combination.

1. Arrange sliced almonds in a fleur-de-lis design around the perimeter of the cake. Use four slices to make a flower design in the center of the cake.

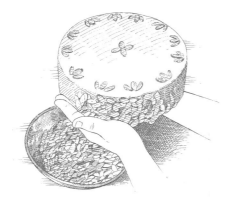

2. To press nuts onto the sides of the cake, lift the cake off the stand or counter and hold it by the cardboard round underneath. Use one hand to hold the cake above a bowl containing nuts; use the other hand to press the nuts into the icing, letting the excess fall back into the bowl. You will need about one cup of nuts to cover the sides of a 9-inch layer cake. You can use sliced almonds (as pictured) or chopped pecans or walnuts.

Number 76

Cakes: *Decorating* | USING JAR LIDS TO MAKE A TWO-TONE PATTERN

Powdered sugar and cocoa powder can be used singly or in combination to give a frosted cake a polished look. When using stencils of any sort, freeze the cake for 15 minutes before decorating. Powdered sugar will gradually dissolve, so apply this fancy decoration just before serving.

1. Gather six jar lids, varying in size from small to medium. Place the lids face down on the surface of the cake in a random arrangement, letting some hang over the edge. Dust the cake with cocoa or confectioners' sugar.

2. Remove the lids, grasping them by the lip and lifting straight up. Rearrange them randomly again, then dust with a contrasting color, using confectioners' sugar, cocoa, or very finely ground nuts. Remove the lids carefully.

Number 77

Cakes: *Decorating* | APPLYING CHOCOLATE SHAVINGS

If the chocolate is too hard, it can be difficult to pull off thick shavings. Even if you do cut off nice shavings, warmth from your fingers can cause the pieces to melt as you try to place them on the cake. Here's how to avoid both problems.

1. Warm a block of bittersweet or semisweet chocolate by sweeping a hair dryer over it, taking care not to melt the chocolate. Holding a paring knife at a 45-degree angle against the chocolate, scrape toward you, anchoring the block with your other hand.

2. Pick up the shavings with a toothpick and place them as desired on the frosted cake.

Cakes: *Decorating* | WRITING ON THE FROSTING

There are times when you will want to write a message on top of a frosted cake. It's easiest to use chocolate to write on a light-colored frosting.

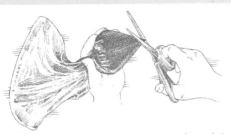

2. Holding the bag in one hand, gently squeeze the chocolate out of the hole as you write.

1. Put semisweet or bittersweet chocolate in a zipper-lock plastic bag and immerse the bag in hot water until the chocolate melts. Dry the bag, then snip off a small piece from one corner.

Cakes: *Decorating* | REMOVING STENCILS

Store-bought stencils (available in most kitchen shops) are an easy way to decorate an unfrosted cake. The problem is removing the stencil without marring the design.

1. Create two handles for the stencil by folding two short lengths of masking tape back on themselves, pinching the middle sections together. Stick the ends of the tape to the top and bottom of the stencil, placing a handle on either side.

2. Place the stencil on the cake and dust with confectioners' sugar or cocoa powder. When you are done, use the tape "handles" to grasp and lift the stencil straight up and off the cake.

Number 80

Cakes: *Decorating* | DUSTING A FLOURLESS CHOCOLATE CAKE

A flourless chocolate cake is rarely frosted, but it can be dressed up a bit with some confectioners' sugar.

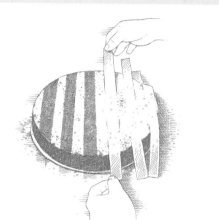

1. Lay strips of paper about ³/₄ inch wide across the top of the cake and then sieve confectioners' sugar over the top.

2. Carefully peel away the paper strips to reveal an attractive striped pattern.

Number 81

Cappuccino | FOAMING MILK ON THE STOVE

Here's how to make steamed, frothy milk for coffee without an expensive espresso machine.

Place a pan filled with heated milk on a potholder or other protective surface and beat the milk with a hand-held electric mixer until the consistency of the milk is foamy and velvety. Milk foamed this way will hold soft peaks, even when spooned into coffee mugs.

Carrots | CUTTING INTO JULIENNE

The term "julienne," which usually applies to vegetables, means to cut into long, thin strips. It can be tricky to figure out how to julienne long, thin vegetables such as carrots, zucchini, or parsnips.

1. Start by slicing the vegetables on the bias into rounds about $1/4$ inch thick and 2 inches long.

2. Fan out several rounds and cut them into $1/4$ inch strips. This shape is sometimes called the matchstick cut.

Number 83

Cauliflower | CUTTING INTO FLORETS

Here's an easy way to cut a head of cauliflower into neat florets. Start by pulling off and discarding the outer leaves.

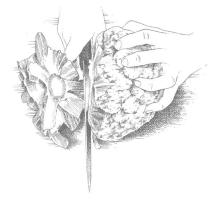

1. Turn the cauliflower on its side and cut off the stem near the base of the head with a chef's knife.

2. Turn the cauliflower so the stem end is facing up. Using a small chef's knife or large paring knife, cut around the core to remove it.

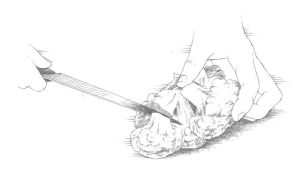

3. Separate the individual florets from the inner stem using the tip of a chef's knife.

4. Cut the florets in half or in quarters, as necessary, to yield pieces of the desired size.

Number 84

Celery | CHOPPING QUICKLY

Recipes often call for a small amount of chopped celery. Rather than breaking off one or more ribs and ending up with too much, try this method.

With a chef's knife, chop the entire bunch across the top. It is easier to get just the amount you need, and the whole bunch gets shorter as you use it, so it's easier to store.

Number 85

Celery Root | REMOVING THE THICK PEEL

Celery root is covered with a thick, hairy skin that can't be removed with a vegetable peeler. Because it's round and too large to hold in your hand, using a paring knife can be tricky. Here's how to cut away the peel safely.

Cut off about $3/8$ inch from the root end (where there is a mass of rootlets) and the stalk end (the opposite side). The celery root can now rest flat on a cutting board. To peel, simply cut from top to bottom, rotating the celery root as you remove wide strips of skin.

Number 86

Cheese | SLICING GOAT CHEESE

A knife quickly becomes covered with this soft cheese, making it difficult to cut clean, neat slices. Here's how to avoid this sticky situation.

Slide an 18-inch piece of dental floss under a log of goat cheese. Cross the ends of the floss above the cheese and then pull the floss through the cheese to make slices. Move the floss and cut again to make slices of the desired thickness.

Number 87

Cheese | SLICING MOZZARELLA

Fresh mozzarella cheese should be quite soft, which makes it difficult to slice neatly with a knife. Here's a neater, faster way to slice fresh mozzarella.

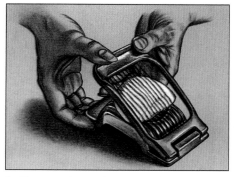 

1. Place a piece of mozzarella in an egg slicer. Close the egg slicer to cut through the cheese.

2. Remove the cheese from the egg slicer and separate the individual slices.

Number 88

Cheese | CRUMBLING BLUE CHEESE

You can crumble blue cheese by hand, but that method can produce pieces of varying sizes.

For more evenly sized pieces (which is a plus in blue cheese dressing and other recipes where the cheese is not cooked), use a fork to crumble the cheese.

Number 89

Cheese | SHREDDING SEMISOFT CHEESE NEATLY

Semisoft cheeses such as cheddar or commercial mozzarella can stick to a box grater and cause a real mess. Here's how to keep the holes on the grater from becoming clogged.

1. Use nonstick cooking spray to lightly coat the coarse side of the box grater.

2. Shred the cheese as usual. The cooking spray will keep the cheese from sticking to the surface of the grater.

Number 90

Cheese |
GRATING HARD CHEESE NEATLY

A box grater often creates a mess on the counter, and you end up losing a lot of the Parmesan or other grating cheese in the process. Here's how to grate more efficiently and neatly.

1. Wrap a piece of plastic wrap around the bottom of the grater and secure it with a rubber band.

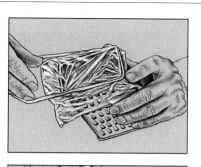

2. Grate the cheese as usual, allowing the grated bits to become trapped by the plastic. When you think you have enough cheese, loosen the rubber band and place the plastic wrap, with the grated cheese, on the counter. If you need to measure the cheese, simply fold the wrap in half and pour the cheese into a measuring cup.

Number 91

Cherries | PITTING THREE WAYS

Cherry pitters work well, but not every cook has one on hand. Here are some techniques you can use to pit cherries without a specialized tool. Always work over a bowl to catch the juices.

A. Push the cherry firmly down onto the pointed, jagged end of a pastry bag tip. Take care not to cut your fingers on the points as they pierce the fruit.

B. Pierce the skin at the stem end with a pair of clean needle-nose pliers. Spread the pliers just enough to grasp the pit, and pull it straight out.

C. Push a drinking straw through the bottom of the cherry, forcing the pit up and out through the stem end.

Number 92

Chicken|CONTAINING RAW CHICKEN

The possibility of raw chicken contaminating any surface it touches is a real concern. It can be especially tricky to avoid cross-contamination when washing and drying chicken before it is cooked. The slippery chicken can slide right off a cutting board onto the counter or soak through any number of protective layers of paper towel. Here's a good way to keep the bird contained as you wash and dry it.

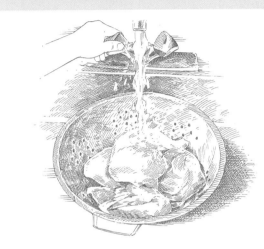

Set the raw chicken in a metal colander while washing it. You can also pat the chicken dry while it's still in the colander. When done, simply transfer the chicken to a roasting pan or cooking vessel. Remember to wash your hands and the colander with hot, soapy water. The colander can even go into the dishwasher.

Number 93

Chicken|SEASONING THE BIRD WITH LEMON

The flavor of lemon is lovely with chicken or turkey, but squeezing a lemon half or pouring lemon juice into the cavity of a bird can result in a messy spill. Here's how to limit the mess and maximize the amount of lemon juice that actually goes into the bird.

Choose a thin-skinned or somewhat older, more pliable lemon. Cut the lemon in half and turn the halves inside out. It's now easy to rub the cavity evenly and neatly with lemon juice.

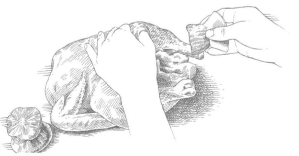

Number 94

Chicken | MEASURING THE INTERNAL TEMPERATURE

When trying to figure out if a chicken is done, we recommend that you use an instant-read thermometer. Be sure to put the thermometer into the thickest part of the bird and avoid all bones, which can throw off your reading.

1. To take the temperature of the thigh, insert the thermometer at an angle into the area between the drumstick and breast. Dark meat tastes best cooked to 165 or 170 degrees.

2. To take the temperature of the breast, insert the thermometer from the neck end, holding it parallel to the bird. The breast meat is done at 160 degrees and will begin to dry out at higher temperatures.

Number 95

Chicken | BUTTERFLYING FOR FASTER COOKING

A whole small chicken takes an hour or more to roast. If you are in hurry, you can butterfly the chicken (basically, you are opening the bird up so it forms a single, flat piece of meat) to shave at least 20 minutes off the cooking time. A butterflied chicken can also be grilled or broiled.

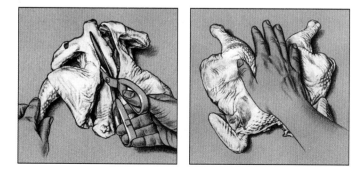

1. With poultry shears, cut through the bones on either side of the backbone, then remove and discard the backbone.

2. Turn the chicken over and use the heel of your hand to flatten the breastbone.

Number 96

Chicken: *Cutlets* | TRIMMING FAT AND TENDONS

Boneless, skinless chicken cutlets are the ultimate convenience food. For the best results, however, take a few minutes to cut away excess fat and tendons that will be unpleasant to eat.

1. Lay each cutlet tenderloin-side down (the tenderloin is that floppy, thin piece of meat attached to the breast), and smooth the top with your fingers. Any yellow fat will slide to the periphery, where it can be trimmed with a knife.

2. To remove the tough, white tendon, turn the cutlet tenderloin-side up and peel back the thick half of the tenderloin so it lies top down on the work surface. Use the point of a paring knife to cut around the tip of the tendon to expose it, then scrape the tendon free with the knife.

Number 97

Chicken: *Cutlets* | SAUTÉING SAFELY

Hot fat can splash hands and arms when cold cutlets are added to a skillet. Here's how to minimize that risk.

Lay the cutlet into the pan thick side first and hang onto the tapered end until the whole cutlet is in the pan. The tapered ends of the cutlets should be at the edges of the pan, where the heat is less intense and where they will cook a bit more slowly than the thick middle portions.

Number 98

Chicken: *Cutlets* | POUNDING CUTLETS

For some dishes, you may want to pound cutlets until they are thin. This is especially important when breading cutlets. The thicker the cutlet, the more time it needs in the pan, and the more time it spends in the pan, the more likely the breading is to burn. The problem is that by the time you get thick cutlets thin enough, they may be ragged pieces of meat so large they won't fit in a skillet. Here's how to minimize the pounding to produce good-looking cutlets that are thin but not excessively large.

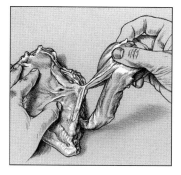

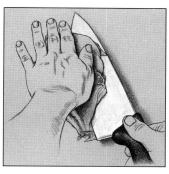

1. The tenderloins (the long, narrow piece of meat attached to the breast) tend to fall off during pounding, so they are best removed and reserved for another use, such as a stir-fry.

2. Halve the breasts horizontally to form two cutlets. This minimizes the amount of pounding necessary.

3. Place the breasts, smooth side down, on a large sheet of plastic wrap. Cover with a second sheet of plastic and pound gently. The cutlets should already be thin; you simply want to make sure they have the same thickness from end to end.

Number 99

Chicken: *Cutlets* | MESS-FREE BREADING

Dipping pounded cutlets into a bowl of beaten eggs and then bread crumbs can be messy. Before you know it, your fingers—not the cutlets—are coated with crumbs. This tip works equally well with turkey or veal cutlets, or fish fillets, such as flounder.

1. Use a pair of tongs to dip each cutlet into the bowl with the beaten eggs.

2. Use the tongs to transfer the cutlets to a pie plate filled with bread crumbs or cornmeal. Press the crumbs lightly onto the cutlets with your fingertips to ensure that the crumbs adhere to the surface of the food. Because your fingers were never in the bowl with the eggs, they should remain dry and crumb-free.

Number 100

Chicken: *Cutlets* | KEEPING BREADING FIRMLY ATTACHED

There's nothing worse than breading that comes off when cutlets are cooked. Here's how to prevent this from happening with chicken, veal, or turkey cutlets.

Transfer the breaded cutlets to a baking rack set over a baking sheet. Allow the cutlets to dry for 5 minutes. This brief drying time stabilizes the coating so that it won't stick to the pan or fall off.

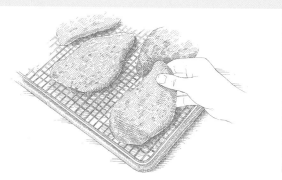

Number 101

Chicken: *Cutlets* | CUTTING INTO UNIFORM PIECES

When stir-frying or making pot pies, it's nice to have uniform pieces of chicken breast that will cook at the same rate. Here's how to turn an ungainly cutlet into neat, even strips of meat. It's easiest to cut the cutlet when it is has been partially frozen for an hour or so.

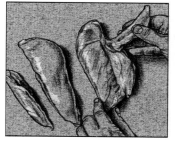

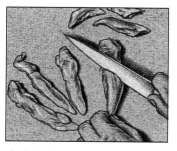

1. Separate the tenderloins (the long, floppy pieces of meat) from the breasts and set them aside.

2. Slice the breasts across the grain into long, thin strips. Center pieces need to be cut in half so that they are approximately the same length as end pieces.

3. Cut the tenderloins on the diagonal to produce pieces the same size as the strips of breast meat.

Number 102

Chicken: *Cutlets* | STABILIZING STUFFED CHICKEN BREASTS

Stuffed chicken dishes, such as chicken Kiev, require long skewers that seal the meat and keep the cheese safely inside. Toothpicks are not long enough, and most cooks don't have the long metal skewers used by restaurants. Here's an easy solution every cook can use.

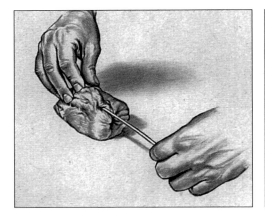

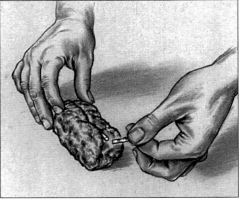

1. Stuff the breast, then pin it together by pushing an uncooked spaghetti noodle through the meat.

2. After the breast has cooked, break off the blackened end of the noodle. The part of the noodle that remains inside the chicken will have cooked through in the chicken juices and won't interfere with the taste of the chicken.

Number 103

Chicken: *Parts* | SEPARATING THE THIGH FROM THE DRUMSTICK

Whole legs are readily available and inexpensive, but they can be difficult to cook and eat. Here's how to separate them neatly.

A thin joint connects the drumstick to the thigh. If you can find the joint, it's easy to cut them apart. Miss the joint and even the sharpest knife may get stuck in bone. Luckily, a line of fat runs right over the joint. Simply turn the leg skin-side down and locate the line of fat that separates the drumstick from the thigh. With a large chef's knife, cut down through the fat and the joint that lies below to separate the two pieces.

Number 104

Chicken: *Parts* | QUICK SKINNING

You may want to remove the fat from chicken parts before cooking them. For instance, we don't miss the skin when oven-frying or pan-frying chicken parts. The coating adds plenty of crunch and the skin is often flabby and unappetizing. Here's how to remove the skin easily and quickly. This tip is especially helpful when skinning legs.

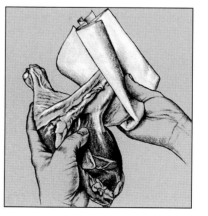

Grasp the skin with a paper towel so it doesn't slip out of your fingers, then gently tug until the skin pulls away and separates from the meat.

Number 105

Chicken: *Parts* | GRILLING BONE-IN BREASTS

Everyone loves grilled bone-in, skin-on breasts. But all too often the exterior burns before the meat in thick breasts is fully cooked. Here's how to make sure the meat near the bone is done without causing the skin to burn. You can use this same trick to finish cooking thick chops.

Once the chicken is nicely browned and nearly done, slide the pieces to a cool part of the grill and cover them with a disposable aluminum roasting pan. The pan traps the heat to create an oven-like effect on your grill. While the meat continues to cook, the skin won't color any further.

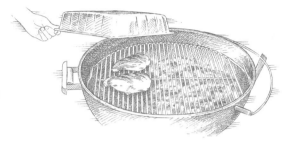

Number 106

Chicken: *Parts* | REMOVING THE WINGS WITHOUT BREAST MEAT

Many people won't eat the wings, so why not cut them off before cooking the bird and save them to make stock? Depending on your technique, you can pull off quite a lot of meat along with the wing, which seems like a shame if the wing is just going into the stockpot. Here's how to remove a wing without taking a piece of the breast with it.

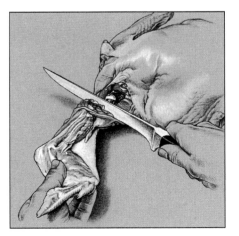

Place the chicken breast-side down and expose the joint that connects the wing to the breast. With a sharp knife, cut right through the joint and separate the wing from the rest of the chicken.

Number 107

Chicken: *Parts* | GETTING WINGS READY TO COOK

While some people can't stand wings, others just love them and buy wings especially for grilling or roasting. Even wing lovers will admit that eating this jointed piece of meat can be messy. To minimize the mess, we like to separate the three sections of the wing before cooking.

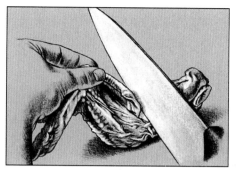

1. With a chef's knife, cut into the skin between the two larger sections of the wing until you hit the joint.

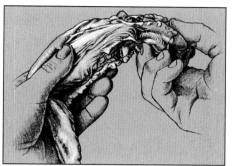

2. Bend back the two sections to pop and break the joint.

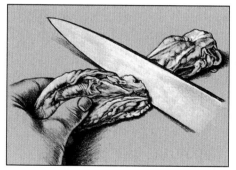

3. Cut through the skin and flesh to completely separate the two meaty portions.

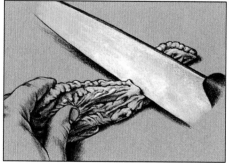

4. One portion will contain the thin wingtip, which has absolutely no meat. We hack off the wingtip and either discard or save it for stock. The two remaining pieces are small enough to be eaten as finger food and much less awkward to hold.

Number 108

Chiles | FREEZING CHIPOTLE CHILES IN ADOBO SAUCE

Chipotles (smoked, dried jalapeño chiles) are among our favorite chiles because they are so flavorful. Chipotles are often packed in adobo sauce (a vinegary tomato sauce flavored with garlic) and canned. Because a little bit of chipotle chile goes a long way, it can be difficult to use up an entire can once it has been opened. Rather than letting the remaining chiles go bad in the refrigerator, try this trick. We like to preserve tomato paste in the same fashion.

1. Spoon out the chipotles, each with a couple of teaspoons of adobo sauce, onto different areas of a cookie sheet lined with parchment or waxed paper. Place the cookie sheet in the freezer.

2. Once frozen, the chipotles should be transferred to a zipper-lock plastic bag and stored in the freezer. You can remove them, one at a time, as needed. They will keep indefinitely.

Number 109

Chocolate | MELTING IN A DRIP COFFEE MACHINE

A microwave, set at 50 percent power, is a great place to melt chocolate, but not everyone has a microwave. Here's an equally simple and ingenious tip. Whatever you do, don't melt plain chocolate on the stovetop. The heat is too intense, and the chocolate will likely burn.

Roughly chop the chocolate and place it in a small, heatproof bowl. Cover the top of the bowl with plastic, being careful not to bring the plastic too far down the sides of the bowl. Place the bowl on the burner plate of an electric drip coffee machine, turn on the coffee maker, and let the gentle heat of the burner melt the chocolate without scorching it.

Number 110

Cinnamon Rolls | CUTTING FILLED ROLLS WITH DENTAL FLOSS

A knife can squish and tear soft yeast doughs, causing the filling to leak out the sides. Here's how to cut the dough for cinnamon rolls quickly and safely.

Hold a piece of dental floss in either hand and carefully saw through the dough with the floss to separate individual pieces.

Number 111

Clams | SCRUBBING WITH A BRUSH

Many recipes instruct the cook to scrub clams and other shellfish. Don't skip this step; many clams and mussels have bits of sand embedded in the shell that can mar a sauce.

Use a soft brush, sometimes sold in kitchen shops as a vegetable brush, to scrub clams under cold, running water.

Number 112

Clams | STRAINING PRECIOUS LIQUID

Clams (as well as mussels) are often steamed with a little wine and herbs in a covered pot. The cooking liquid is delicious but sometimes gritty. Here's how to remove the grit. (Note that bits of garlic, shallots, and herbs will be lost when the liquid is strained, but their flavors remain in the liquid.)

Pour the cooking liquid through a sieve lined with a single paper towel and set over a measuring cup. If desired, moisten the towel first so that it does not absorb any precious clam juices.

Number 113

Coffee | EFFICIENT GRINDING

Many inexpensive blade-type grinders grind coffee beans unevenly, producing some powder as well as some larger pieces of bean. Here's how to even out the grind.

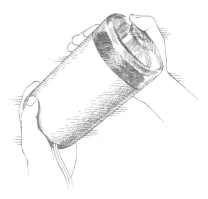

With your hand over the hopper, lift the whole unit off the counter and shake it gently as it grinds. (The motion is akin to blending a martini in a cocktail shaker.) By moving the beans around, you help the machine grind more evenly.

Number 114

Coffee Cakes | DRIZZLING WITH WHITE ICING

The lines of white icing that adorn many coffee cakes are nothing more than sifted confectioners' sugar thinned with a little milk and flavored with a splash of vanilla. Here's how to drizzle the icing over a cooled coffee cake in nice thin lines. Use this tip to decorate molasses-spice cookies, too.

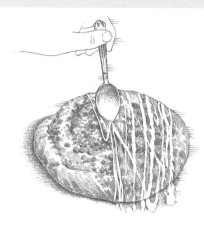

Dip a large dinner spoon into the bowl with the icing. Quickly move the spoon back and forth over the coffee cake, letting the icing fall in thin ribbons from the end of the spoon. Keep dipping the spoon back into the bowl of icing until the coffee cake is amply iced.

Number 115

Cookies | DISTRIBUTING GOODIES EVENLY IN DOUGH

The last few cookies from a batch of chocolate chip cookies never seem to have as many chips as the first few cookies. The same thing often happens with nuts and raisins. Here's how to avoid this common problem.

Reserve some of the chips, nuts, or other goodies and mix them into the dough after about half of it has been scooped out for cookies. This way, the last of the cookies will have as much good stuff as the first batch.

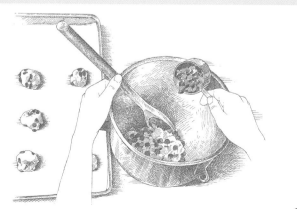

Number 116

Cookies | MAKING EVEN-SIZED BALLS OF DOUGH

For the best-looking cookies, it is important to start with balls of dough that are all the same size. Many recipes suggest rolling the dough into balls of a specific diameter, but it's difficult to measure the balls with a ruler set on the counter. Here's how to get an accurate measurement.

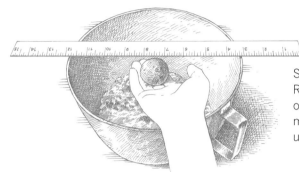

Set the ruler on top of the bowl. Rather than placing the ball of dough on top of the ruler (where it's hard to measure the equator), bring the ball up along the side of the ruler.

Number 117

Cookies | MEASURING OUT STICKY DOUGH

Some cookie dough can be so sticky that your hands become a mess in no time. Here's a neat way to get balls of dough that are all the same size without soiling your hands.

Use a small ice cream scoop to measure out the dough. Dip the scoop into cold water between scoopings to ensure that the dough releases easily every time.

Number 118

Cookies | FREEZING DOUGH

Keeping frozen dough on hand means you can bake just as many, or as few, cookies as you like without first having to whip up a batch of dough. Most cookie doughs can withstand a month or so in the freezer.

Form the dough into balls and arrange them on a cookie sheet lined with parchment or waxed paper. Place the cookie sheet in the freezer. When the balls of dough are frozen, place them in a zipper-lock plastic bag or small airtight container. When you want to make cookies, remove as many balls as you like and bake as directed, increasing the cooking time by a minute or two.

Number 119

Cookies | SLICING ICEBOX COOKIES

Logs of dough stored in the freezer are great to have on hand, but we've noticed that the dough can soften by the time you get to the end, making it difficult to get neat slices. Here's how to prevent this problem.

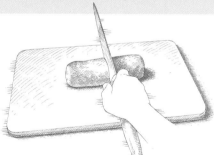

1. When you are ready to bake cookies, remove the dough log from the freezer and cut it into short lengths, no more than 3 inches long. Place all but one piece of dough back in the freezer.

2. Using a very sharp chef's knife, slice the piece of dough left out. To prevent one side of the log from flattening due to the pressure you put on it, roll the dough an eighth of a turn after every slice. Once this first piece of dough has been completely sliced, retrieve the next piece from the freezer and slice in the same manner.

Number 120

Cookies | REUSING THE SAME BAKING SHEET

Baking batch after batch of cookies can be a frustrating exercise, especially when you have only one cookie sheet. No one wants to scrub the same baking sheet many times, but dough balls must be placed on a clean surface. Here's how to work quickly and efficiently when you have just one cookie sheet.

1. Load up a sheet of parchment paper with balls of dough, slide the paper onto the cookie sheet, and place the cookies in the oven.

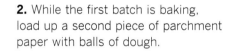

2. While the first batch is baking, load up a second piece of parchment paper with balls of dough.

3. When the baked cookies come out of the oven, whisk the parchment and its cargo onto a cooling rack. After cooling the baking sheet with a quick rinse and dry, it's ready for the next prepared batch.

Number 121

Cookies | SHAPING THUMBPRINTS

The best thumbprints have a deep, round indentation to hold the dollop of jam or chocolate securely. Your thumb can be used to make a deep indentation, but not a round one. Here's how we like to shape these cookies.

Press the back side of a melon baller (which is usually perfectly round) into dough balls before baking. The end of a wooden honey dipper is also well suited to this task.

Number 122

Cookies | SHAPING SUGAR COOKIES

Sugar cookies have two distinctive features—they should have an even thickness from side to side and they must be lightly coated with granulated sugar. Here's how to accomplish both goals with one motion.

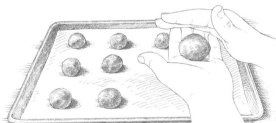

1. Take a piece of dough and roll it between your palms into a ball. (Our favorite size sugar cookie starts with 1½ tablespoons of dough formed into balls about 1½ inches in diameter.) Roll the ball of dough in a bowl filled with granulated sugar.

2. Choose a drinking glass that measures about 2 inches across the bottom. Butter the bottom of the glass and dip it into a bowl of sugar. Use the glass to flatten the dough balls. To make sure that the cookies are nicely coated with sugar, dip the glass back into the bowl of sugar after shaping every other cookie.

Number 123

Cookies | SHAPING LACE COOKIES PERFECTLY

Lifting lace cookies off the pan and shaping them before they harden and become brittle requires exact timing. The method we use makes it easy to lift the cookies while still hot. It also eliminates the need to move the hot cookies off the baking sheet with a spatula, a process that often results in torn or bunched-up cookies.

1. Line up four upside-down ramekins or small bowls. Then cut a sheet of parchment paper to fit the baking pan, and cut that sheet into four equal pieces.

2. Drop one tablespoon of batter onto the center of each piece of parchment and bake.

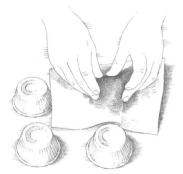

3. When the cookies come out of the oven, lift one of the parchment squares off the sheet and onto a plate to cool, leaving the other three on the hot pan to keep them warm and pliable. Cool the cookie on the plate to the right consistency for molding (this takes 30 to 60 seconds).

4. Pick up the parchment square, turn the cookie over, and lay it on the bottom of the ramekin or bowl to shape it. Lift the parchment from the cookie. Repeat steps 3 and 4 with the other three cookies. Cool the cookies completely before lifting them off the ramekins or bowls.

Cookies|SUGARING CRESCENT COOKIES

Almond crescents as well as butterballs or Mexican wedding cakes should have a thick, even coating of confectioners' sugar. Many recipes suggest sugaring the cookies as soon as they come out of the oven. Although the coating adheres well to warm cookies, the sugar often tastes pasty because it has melted a bit. Here's how to ensure that the coating is thick but never pasty.

Once the cookies have cooled, roll them in a bowl of confectioners' sugar and shake off the excess. Don't worry if the coating is spotty in places; just go ahead and store the cookies in an airtight container. When ready to serve, roll the cookies in sugar again to cover any blemishes.

Cookies|USING GINGERBREAD PEOPLE AS DECORATIONS

Many bakers like to hang decorated gingerbread people from the Christmas tree. If you make a hole in the dough before baking, it closes up. Waiting until after the baked cookie has cooled can cause the cookie to break apart. Here's how to punch out a hole safely.

As soon as you remove the baked cookies from the oven, use a drinking straw to poke a hole near the top of each one. The holes won't change shape as the cookies cool.

91

Number 126

Cookies | MAKING YOUR OWN COLORED SUGAR

Colored sugar makes a fine decoration for holiday cookies. However, many stores carry just one or two colors, and you often end up with more than you need. Here's how to customize your colors and make only as much as you need.

1. Sprinkle about ½ cup granulated sugar evenly over the bottom of a pie plate or metal bowl. Add about five drops of food coloring and mix thoroughly.

2. To be sure the color is evenly distributed, push the sugar through a fine sieve. Spread the sugar back on the pie plate or on a baking sheet and let dry completely.

Number 127

Cookies | ORGANIZING COOKIE DECORATIONS

During the holiday season you may be decorating cookies several times. Here's a good way to organize your favorite decorations. If you have kids, you'll also appreciate this neat way to organize colored sugar, sprinkles, and such.

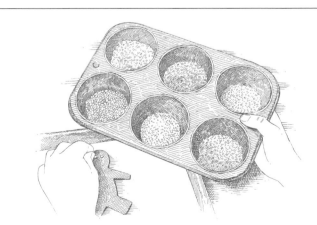

Place a different decoration in each cup of a muffin tin, which is easy to move around the kitchen and store for next time.

Number 128

Cooking Fat|EASY DISPOSAL

Excess fat from cooked bacon, sausage, or ground meat can clog pipes. Here's an easy way to get rid of this fat.

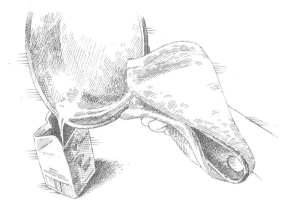

Wash out empty heavy-duty cardboard containers from half-and-half or heavy cream and save them under the sink. When you have some hot bacon or other fat to throw away, pull out one of the stored cartons and pour it in. Once the fat has cooled, close the carton and dispose of it.

Number 129

Cooking Spray|NO-MESS SPRAYING

Many cooks have encountered the oily film on their counter or workspace that results from using an aerosol nonstick cooking spray. Here's how to avoid this problem.

Open the dishwasher door, lay the item to be greased right on the door, and spray away. Any excess or over-spray will be cleaned off the door the next time you run the dishwasher.

Number 130

Cookware | PROTECTING NONSTICK PANS

The surfaces on nonstick pans can chip or scratch easily, especially if you stack pans in a cabinet. Here's how to store them efficiently and safely.

Place a doubled sheet of paper towel between each pan as you nest the pans in a stack.

Number 131

Cookware | LIFTING HOT LIDS

Rather than burning your fingers or searching around for a potholder every time you want to lift a lid off a pot on the stove, try this tip.

Before cooking, wedge a wine cork under the handle of the lid. The cork stays cool when the lid gets hot, giving you something safe to grab onto when lifting the lid.

Number 132

Cookware | KEEPING TRACK OF POT LIDS

Most cooks throw all their lids into one drawer, making it hard to match the right lid with the right pan. Here are two ways to keep your lids organized.

A. If you store your pans in a cabinet, set an adjustable V-rack for roasting to the widest setting, and stand the lids up in the slots between the wires of the rack.

B. If you hang your pans from hooks, slide the loop handle of the lid right onto the handle of its matching pan, then hang the pan from the hook.

Number 133

Cookware | CLEANING COPPER

Copper cookware looks great but is notorious for tarnishing quickly. Commercial copper polish requires some scrubbing and costs a lot of money. Here's a way to save money and work.

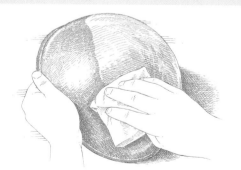

1. With a paper towel, smear a thin layer of ketchup over the tarnished surface.

2. Wait five minutes, then wipe and rinse the ketchup off. The acidity in the ketchup lifts the tarnish away.

Number 134

Corn | BUTTERING CORN AND BREAD TOGETHER

Using a knife to butter an ear of corn can be messy and frustrating, as the melting butter slides off the knife and down the ear. Here's an easier way to butter corn.

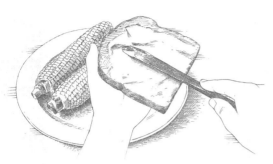 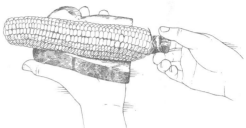

1. If serving sliced bread with dinner, spread a thick layer of butter on the bread.

2. Hold the bread in one hand and roll the hot ear of corn over the buttered bread, evenly coating the corn with butter.

Number 135

Corn | REMOVING THE KERNELS

Cutting the kernels from long ears of corn can be tricky. Tapered ears wobble on cutting boards, and kernels can go flying around the kitchen. Here's a way to work safely and more neatly.

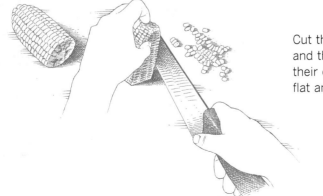

Cut the ear in half crosswise and then stand the half ears on their cut surfaces, which are flat and stable.

Number 136

Corn | PREPARING CORN FOR GRILLING

Adding flavor from the grill is a nice but tricky thing to do with fresh corn. Husked ears tend to burn, and unhusked ears steam on the grill, failing to pick up that great smoky flavor. Here's how to keep corn from burning and infuse it with grilled flavor.

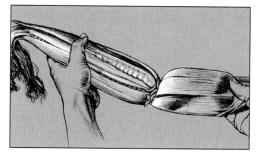

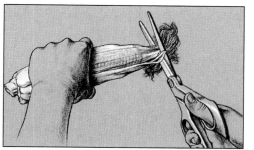

1. Before grilling, remove all but the inner-most layer of husk.

2. Use scissors to snip off the tassel. The ear can now be grilled without soaking or further preparation. When done (see next tip), simply peel back the remaining husk and serve.

Number 137

Corn | TELLING WHEN GRILLED CORN IS DONE

When boiling corn, most cooks know how long they like to keep it in the water. Timing can be tricky when grilling corn, especially since fires vary in intensity. If you prepare corn according to the method outlined in the previous tip, there's a visual clue you can use to judge when the corn is tender.

As soon as the husk picks up the dark silhouette of kernels and begins to pull away from the tip of the ear, the corn is ready to come off the grill.

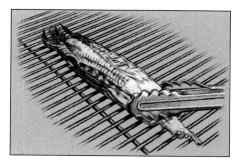

Number 138

Cornish Hens | PRICKING SKIN TO PREVENT BALLOONING

When roasted whole, juices inside a Cornish hen can build up and cause the skin to balloon. Here's how to prevent this unsightly occurrence.

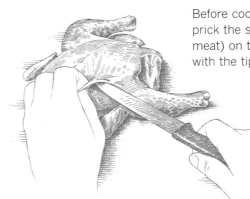

Before cooking, carefully prick the skin (but not the meat) on the breast and leg with the tip of a knife.

Number 139

Crabs | CLEANING SOFT-SHELLS

Although your fishmonger will probably offer to clean soft-shell crabs for you, for optimum freshness you should clean the crabs yourself, right before cooking.

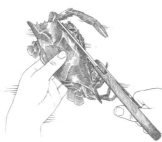

1. Start by cutting off the mouth with kitchen shears; the mouth is the first part of the shell to harden. You can also cut off the eyes at the same time, but this is purely for aesthetic reasons since the eyes are edible.

2. Lift the pointed side of the crab and cut out the spongy off-white gills underneath; the gills are fibrous and watery and unpleasant to eat.

3. Finally, turn the crab on its back and cut off the triangular, or T-shaped, "apron flap" at the tail.

Number 140

Crackers | CREATING A VACUUM SEAL

Nothing's worse than stale, soggy crackers. Here's how to make zipper-lock bags more effective.

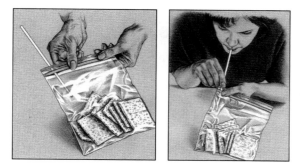

1. Put the crackers in the bag and insert a straw at one side. Seal the bag around the straw.

2. Suck out as much air as possible through the straw, then remove the straw and finish sealing the bag.

Number 141

Cream | CHILLING THE BOWL WITHOUT USING THE FREEZER

For the best results, you should chill a bowl before whipping cream in it. For many cooks, the freezer is either too small or too full to accommodate a large bowl. Here's how to chill the bowl in the refrigerator.

1. At least 15 minutes before whipping the cream, fill the bowl with ice cubes and cold water, place the whisk in the ice water (it helps to chill this as well), and put the bowl into the refrigerator.

2. When ready to whip the cream, dump out the ice water, dry the bowl and whisk, and add the cream. The bowl will stay cold as you work, and the cream whips up beautifully.

Number 142

Cream | JUDGING WHEN CREAM IS PROPERLY WHIPPED

Many recipes instruct the cook to whip cream to either soft or stiff peaks. Here's an easy way to tell when you should stop beating.

1. Cream whipped to soft peaks will droop slightly from the ends of the beaters.

2. Cream whipped to stiff peaks will cling tightly to the ends of the beaters and hold its shape.

Number 143

Cucumbers | SEEDING

In many recipes, the watery seeds are removed from cucumbers. Here's an easy way to accomplish this task.

Halve the cucumber (already peeled if desired) lengthwise. Run a small spoon inside each cucumber half to scoop out the seeds and surrounding liquid.

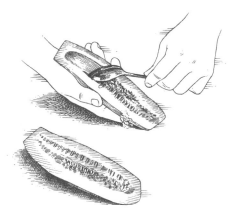

Cucumbers | WEIGHTING

Even when seeded, cucumbers can give off a lot of liquid and make dressings too watery. For this reason, we think it's a good idea to salt and weight cucumbers before dressing them.

1. Lay seeded cucumber halves flat side down on a work surface and slice them on the diagonal into ¼-inch-thick pieces.

2. Toss the cucumbers with salt (one teaspoon for every cucumber) in a colander. To help extract as much liquid as possible, weight the cucumbers. To apply the weight evenly, fill a gallon-sized plastic bag with water and seal tightly. Place the bag over the cucumbers in the colander. Let the cucumbers drain for at least 1 hour, preferably for 3 hours. There's no need to rinse off the salt; just make sure not to add salt to the dressing.

Custard | JUDGING WHEN IT IS DONE

Custards for ice cream and pie fillings must be heated slowly to allow the eggs to thicken the cream and/or milk. If the custard gets too hot, though, the eggs will scramble and the custard will curdle. Here's a simple way to tell when the custard should come off the heat.

Scrape a wooden spatula or spoon along the bottom of the pan. When a bit of custard just begins to adhere to the edge of the spatula, the custard is done.

Number 146

Cutting Board | KEEPING IT STABLE

Chefs put a damp kitchen towel beneath a cutting board to keep it from slipping all over the counter. The problem is that you are left with a damp kitchen towel that needs to be laundered.

Instead of a kitchen towel, lay a damp sheet of paper towel on the counter and then place the cutting board on top. The damp paper towel holds the board in place and can be used to wipe down the counter when you are done and then thrown out.

Number 147

Dumplings | NO-STICK STEAMING

Steamed dumplings often stick to the steamer and tear as you try to remove them. Here's how to prevent this from happening.

Line the steamer basket with sturdy lettuce leaves and then place the dumplings on top of the lettuce. This trick can be used with any steamed pastry item.

Number 148

Eggplant | SLICING FOR GRILLING

Eggplant are often sliced lengthwise for grilling. The outer pieces are covered with skin and won't get those nice grill marks on both sides unless you use this tip, which also works with zucchini.

Use a sharp knife to remove the peel from the outer eggplant slices. Besides creating more attractive grill marks, we find that the flesh cooks better when directly exposed to the heat of the grill.

Number 149

Eggs | BEATING THE WHITES

A standing mixer is the best tool for whipping egg whites. However, it can be difficult to tell when the eggs are properly whipped. Also, the speed of the mixer means that eggs can go from properly whipped to overwhipped in seconds. Here's an easy way to keep from overbeating egg whites. Use the same technique when whipping cream in a standing mixer.

Just before the whites reach the proper consistency, turn off the mixer. Detach the whisk attachment and remove the bowl from the mixer. Use the whisk attachment to make the last few strokes by hand. Be sure to scrape along the bottom of the bowl where the whisk may not have reached.

Number 150

Eggs | SEPARATING YOLKS FROM WHITES

The traditional method of separating an egg by tossing the yolk back and forth from one shell to the other often results in a pierced yolk. Hands have no sharp edges that can break the yolk. Just make sure to wash your hands well once the eggs are separated.

1. Crack the egg over the bowl that will hold the whites. Place a second bowl nearby for the yolks. Use the thumb of one hand to pull the halves of the shell apart, being careful to keep the yolk fully contained in one of the halves.

2. Separate the shells and allow as much white as possible to drop into the bowl below. Do not pass the yolk from one shell to the other.

3. Instead, pour the yolk and remaining white into the palm of one hand. Open fingers slightly, allowing the white to drop into the bowl below. Place the whole yolk in the second bowl.

Number 151

Eggs|FOLDING IN BEATEN WHITES

Numerous recipes, everything from cakes to soufflés, call for beaten egg whites, which are usually folded into the batter just before it is baked. If you beat the eggs in too vigorously, the cake or soufflé may not rise. If you don't incorporate the eggs properly, you may be left with eggy patches in your baked goods. Here's the best way to fold beaten egg whites into a batter. Start by vigorously stirring a portion of the beaten whites (most recipes will call for a quarter or third of the whites) into the batter. This lightens the texture of the batter so the rest of the whites can be folded in more gently.

1. Scrape the remaining whites into the bowl. Starting at the top of the bowl, use a rubber spatula to cut through the middle of the whites.

2. Turn the edge of the spatula toward you so it moves up the sides of the bowl.

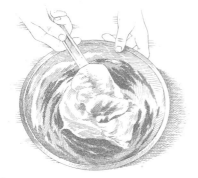

3. Continue this motion, going full circle, until the spatula is back at the center of the bowl again.

4. Follow this procedure four more times, turning the bowl a quarter turn each time. Finally, use the spatula to scrape around the entire circumference of the bowl.

Eggs: *Deviled* | FLUFFY FILLINGS

A pasty, heavy texture in the yolk filling is the downfall of many deviled eggs. Here are two ways to keep the filling light and fluffy.

A. If making many deviled eggs at one time, press the yolks gently through a potato ricer and use a knife to shave the extruded yolk off the bottom of the ricer and into a bowl. The yolks come out smooth, light, and airy.

B. When making smaller batches, grate the yolks using the drum of a Mouli grater. Don't apply too much pressure on the hopper, and the yolks will emerge light and fluffy.

Eggs: *Deviled* | USING A PLASTIC BAG TO FILL EGGS

Once the yolks have been riced or grated and then seasoned, the filling is ready to be piped back into the empty egg halves. A pastry bag fitted with a star tip is the ideal tool for the job. Here's what to do if you don't have a pastry bag.

Spoon the yolk mixture into a plastic bag. Snip a small piece from one bottom corner of the bag and then gently squeeze the filling through the hole into the egg halves.

Number 154

Eggs: *Deviled* | KEEPING FILLED EGGS STABLE FOR TRANSPORT

Preparing beautiful deviled eggs requires care, so it goes without saying that you want them to arrive at your destination looking as perfect as they did in your kitchen. Here's how to keep the eggs upright if you want to bring them in the car.

1. Cut a clean piece of rubberized shelf or drawer liner (available at hardware stores) to the size of the dish you want to use to hold the eggs. Make sure to choose a dish with relatively high sides—a square plastic storage container with a lid is perfect.

2. Lay the fitted liner on the bottom of the container and stock it with enough eggs to fill it in a single layer. The liner keeps the eggs from sliding when the container is moved.

Number 155

Eggs: *Fried* | GETTING THE EGGS INTO THE SKILLET

Fried eggs cook so quickly that seconds can make the difference between a runny yolk and one that has set. If you add the eggs one at a time to a hot pan, the first egg will be done well before the last egg. The problem is keeping track of which egg went into the pan first. Adding all the eggs at exactly the same time means that all the eggs will be done at the same time.

Crack two eggs in two different small bowls. When the pan is ready, slide the eggs from both bowls into the skillet from opposite sides.

Number 156

Eggs: *Hard-Boiled* | IDENTIFYING THEM IN THE REFRIGERATOR

Sometimes it can be difficult to tell which eggs in your refrigerator are raw and which ones are hard-boiled. Here's a simple trick to keep them straight. This only works with white eggs.

Add a little balsamic vinegar to the cooking water along with the eggs. This dark brown vinegar tints the eggshells so you can tell them apart from bright white raw eggs.

Number 157

Eggs: *Hard-Boiled* | PEELING NEATLY

Peeling hard-boiled eggs without gouging the whites can be tricky. Here's how to speed up the process and ensure peeled eggs that look as good as they taste.

 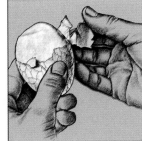

1. Tap the egg all over against the counter surface, then roll it gently back and forth a few times on the counter until cracked all over.

2. Begin peeling from the end with the air pocket so that you can get your fingers under the shell without digging into the egg. The cracked shell should come off in spiral strips attached to the thin membrane.

Number 158

Eggs: *Hard-Boiled* | CUBING PERFECTLY

For egg salad and other dishes, it's nice to have perfect cubes. Hard-boiled eggs are slippery and oddly shaped, so many cooks end up with uneven pieces or, worse, pieces that are slightly mashed. Here's a neat trick that's fast and foolproof.

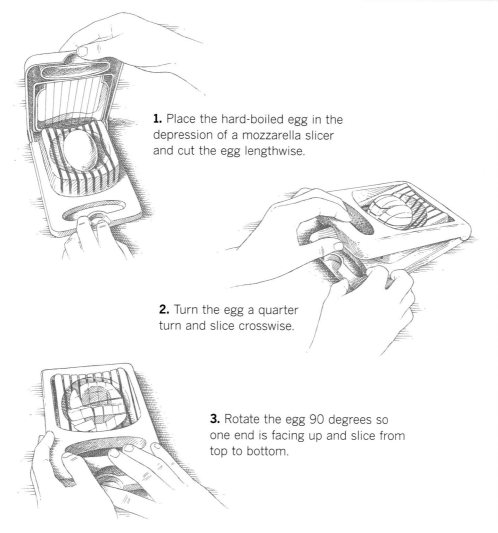

1. Place the hard-boiled egg in the depression of a mozzarella slicer and cut the egg lengthwise.

2. Turn the egg a quarter turn and slice crosswise.

3. Rotate the egg 90 degrees so one end is facing up and slice from top to bottom.

Number 159

Eggs: *Hard-Boiled* | CRUMBLING THE EGG

For garnishes and salads, it is best to use very fine pieces of hard-boiled egg. Chopping the boiled egg can be tricky and usually results in fairly large pieces. Here's a better option.

Press the egg through a mesh sieve to yield fine, even pieces.

Number 160

Eggs: *Poached* | GETTING FOUR EGGS INTO THE WATER SIMULTANEOUSLY

As with frying (see tip 155, page 107), it is important to get all the eggs into the pan at the same time when poaching them. Because there's water in the pan, you must use a slightly different method.

Crack each egg into a small cup with a handle. When the water is ready, lower the lips of each cup into the water at the same time and then tip the eggs into the pan.

Number 161

Extracts | ADDING TINY AMOUNTS

It can be hard to measure small amounts of extracts and food colorings. A baby medicine dropper lets you measure minute amounts and then disperse them evenly over a batter.

Squeeze the rubber bulb on a baby medicine dropper, then dip the tip just below the surface of the liquid in the extract or food coloring bottle. Release the bulb slowly until you have trapped the desired amount of liquid inside the dropper. Squeeze the liquid into the bowl, letting drops fall in various spots on the surface of the batter.

Number 162

Fennel | PREPARING

The bulb is the part of this odd-looking vegetable used in most recipes. Here's how to trim the stalks and remove the tough core from the bulb.

1. Cut off the stems and feathery fronds. (The fronds can be minced and used for garnishing.)

2. Trim a thin slice from the base of the bulb and remove any tough or blemished outer layers of the bulb. Cut the bulb in half through the base and use a paring knife to cut out the pyramid-shaped piece of the core in each half. The fennel bulb can now be sliced or chopped as desired.

Number 163

Fennel Seeds | CHOPPING NEATLY

Small, hard seeds like fennel and cumin are seemingly impossible to chop because they scatter all over the counter when you bear down on them. Here's how to overcome this problem.

1. Place the measured seeds in a small pile on a cutting board. Pour just enough water or oil on the seeds to moisten them.

2. The seeds can now be chopped with a chef's knife and will not fly all over the kitchen.

Number 164

Fish | FREEZING WHOLE FISH

If you like to fish, you know that a good's day catch often must be frozen. Here's how to keep whole fish from getting freezer burn.

1. Partially fill a large zipper-lock plastic bag with cold water. Add the cleaned whole fish.

2. Add more water until the fish is covered. Seal the bag and freeze. Thaw bags in the refrigerator when ready to cook the fish.

Number 165

Fish | SKINNING FILLETS

Removing the skin from fillets can be a tricky job. Here's how to make this task easier.

Starting at the thin end of the fillet, slide a knife between the skin and flesh until you can grab hold of the skin with a paper towel. Use this "handle" to help steady the skin as you continue to cut the flesh away from it.

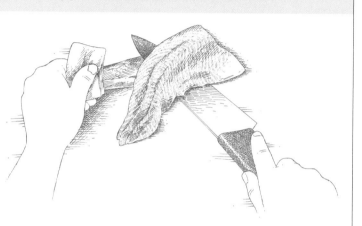

Number 166

Fish | COOKING THIN FILLETS

Many fillets taper down to a thin end, which is prone to overcooking. Here's an easy way to ensure even cooking throughout the fillet.

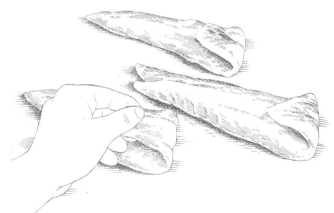

Fold the thin tail piece over so that the fillet is now an even thickness from end to end. Once the tail has been folded, lay the fish into a hot skillet, folded-side up.

Number 167

Flame Tamer | MAKING A FOIL RING

A flame tamer is a metal disk that can be used as a buffer between a burner and a pot in order to maintain a gentle, low level of heat. A flame tamer is especially useful when trying to cook a stew, soup, or sauce at the barest simmer for a long time. Aluminum foil can be fashioned into a thick, slightly flattened ring and placed right on top of a gas burner. By elevating the pot slightly, this makeshift flame tamer reduces the amount of heat that actually reaches the pot.

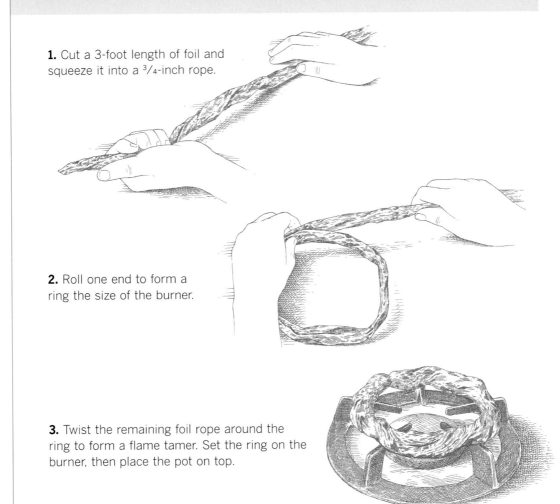

1. Cut a 3-foot length of foil and squeeze it into a ³/₄-inch rope.

2. Roll one end to form a ring the size of the burner.

3. Twist the remaining foil rope around the ring to form a flame tamer. Set the ring on the burner, then place the pot on top.

Number 168

Flour | STORING IN WIDE-MOUTH CONTAINER

This is how we store flours, as well as sugar, in our test kitchen. This tip speeds up the measuring process and keeps our counters clean.

Place flours in wide-mouth plastic containers with airtight lids. When you need to measure flour, simply dip the cup into the flour and then sweep the overflow back into the container.

Number 169

Flour | NO-FUSS FLOURING

Hauling out a large container can be a nuisance when all you have to do is dust a cake pan or work surface with some flour. Use this tip for confectioners' sugar as well.

Set a funnel in an empty glass salt shaker and scoop a little flour into the funnel. When filled, simply seal the shaker and store it in the pantry. These small shakers are easy to reach and do an excellent job of lightly coating a surface with flour.

Number 170

Flour | COATING CUTTERS

Recipes for biscuits and cookies often call for dipping the cutter in flour between cuttings. Here's how we do this in our test kitchen.

Fill the one-cup measure (which is already dirty from measuring flour for the cookies or biscuits) with more flour. As you work, simply dip the cutter right into the measuring cup, which is the perfect shape and size. Best of all, there's no extra bowl to clean up when you are done.

Number 171

Flour | ADDING FLOUR IN INCREMENTS

Many food processor bread recipes call for adding flour in small increments. It can be a real pain to unlock the lid and add flour several times.

Before adding any flour, we shape a doubled piece of parchment or wax paper into a funnel and then slide it into the feed tube of the food processor. Flour can now be added as needed to the funnel, and it will flow slowly, evenly, and steadily into the work bowl.

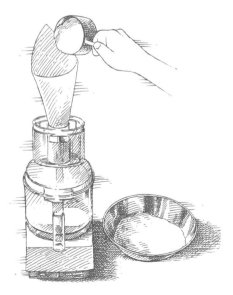

Number 172

Food Processor | KEEPING THE LID CLEAN

Everyone knows that food processors save time in the kitchen, but cleaning them can be a real chore. Here's a neat way to keep the lid clean and thus reduce cleaning time.

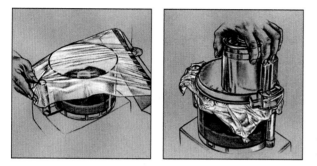

1. Place all ingredients in the work bowl and then cover the bowl with a sheet of plastic wrap.

2. Fit the lid into the work bowl, making sure that the plastic wrap lines the entire lid. Process as directed. When done, simply lift off the clean lid and discard the splattered sheet of plastic.

Number 173

Food Processor | POURING LIQUIDS FROM THE WORK BOWL

Pouring liquids from the work bowl can be tricky. You don't want to remove the blade (and get your hand dirty), but if you don't try something the blade will fall out. Here's how to keep the blade safely in the work bowl as you pour.

1. Remove the work bowl from the food processor when the liquid has been processed. Hold the bowl with one hand and push your finger into the bowl shaft and the hollow of the blade.

2. The bowl can now be turned upside down to pour out the contents while your finger keeps the blade in place.

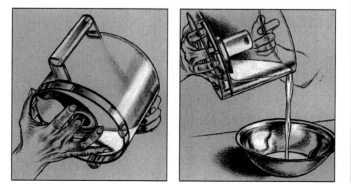

Number 174

Food Processor | CLEANING THE WORK BOWL

The easiest way to clean bowls is to soak them with water prior to washing. However, the hole in the center of a food processor work bowl makes this impossible to do. Here's a way to plug up that hole.

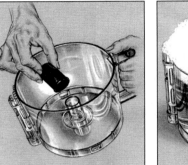

1. Remove the bowl cover and blade. Set an empty 35mm film canister upside down over the hole in the work bowl.

2. Now you can fill the bowl with warm, soapy water and allow it to soak.

Number 175

Freezer | FREEZING SMALLER PORTIONS

For cooks feeding small families, or perhaps just one person, freezing in small batches is a must. Here's a good way to freeze in small batches using large freezersafe plastic bags. Use this technique with chicken cutlets, steaks, or ground meats.

1. Place two portions of food in different locations inside a large zipper-lock freezer bag. Flatten out the bag, forcing air out in the process, so that the portions do not touch.

2. Fold the bag over in the center and freeze. The bag divides the two portions so they will freeze separately. Best of all, you have the choice of using one or both frozen portions.

Number 176

Freezer | KEEPING TRACK OF FROZEN FOODS

Practically every cook with a freezer has put something in there at one point or another only to forget about it completely and throw away the freezer-burned mystery parcel months later. Here's an easy way to keep track of what's in your freezer.

Every time you put something in the freezer, add the name of the food and the date to a list clipped to the freezer door. The list is a constant reminder and will inspire you to use up those frozen goodies.

Number 177

Freezer | FREEING UP CONTAINERS

Plastic food storage containers are at a premium in many kitchens. Unfortunately, many of these containers end up in the freezer for months. Here's how to liberate the containers from the freezer.

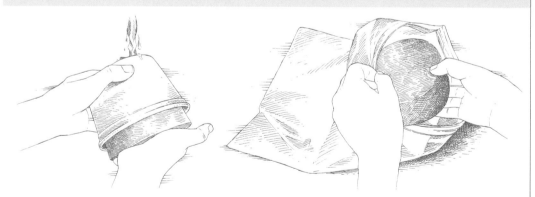

1. Pass the container under hot running water just long enough to release its contents in a frozen block.

2. Drop the frozen block into a zipper-lock freezer bag, seal the bag, and return the food to the freezer.

Number 178

Fruit | CUTTING DRIED FRUIT

Dried fruits, such as peaches, apricots, figs, and dates, are often chopped for use in muffins, cakes, and breads. However, dried fruits are sticky and often adhere to the knife.

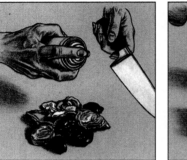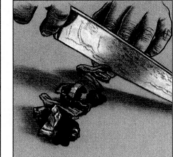

1. Before you start cutting, spray a thin film of vegetable oil onto the blade of your knife.

2. The chopped fruit doesn't cling to the knife blade so you can chop the fruit easily.

Number 179

Garlic | DRY-TOASTING

Here's a simple way to tame that harsh garlic flavor and also loosen the skins for easy peeling. For garlic with a creamier texture (akin to roasted garlic), increase the toasting time to 15 minutes.

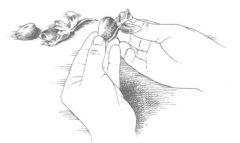

1. Place unpeeled garlic cloves in a dry skillet over medium-high heat. Toast, shaking the pan occasionally, until the skins are golden brown, about 5 minutes. Transfer the toasted cloves to a cutting board and cool.

2. When cooled, the once-clingy skins readily peel off. The garlic can now be sliced, chopped, or minced and used as you normally would, but it will have far less bite.

Number 180

Garlic | PEELING

An old-fashioned rubber jar opener can be used instead of a cannoli-style rubber garlic peeler.

1. Place one or two cloves in the center of the jar opener.

2. Roll the cloves around inside the soft, thin rubber.

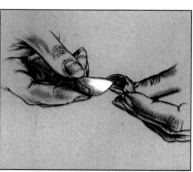

3. The friction created by the rubber will cause the paperlike skin of the garlic to slip right off.

Number 181

Garlic | SEPARATING AND PEELING LARGE AMOUNTS

When a recipe calls for a lot of garlic, separating the individual cloves from the head and then peeling them can be time-consuming. Here's how to save time and work.

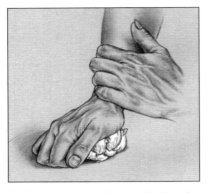

1. Press down on the garlic head with the heel of your hand to loosen the cloves.

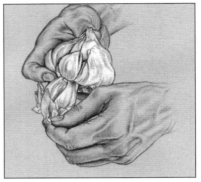

2. Remove as much of the papery skin from the outside of the head as possible.

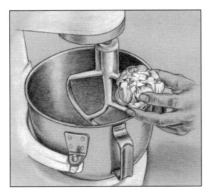

3. Place the head of garlic in a very lightly oiled mixing bowl of an electric mixer and fit the mixer with the paddle attachment.

4. Mix on low speed until the cloves separate and the peels are removed.

Number 182

Garlic | CLEANING A PRESS

Dirty garlic presses are notoriously challenging to clean. Here's an easy way to accomplish this task and recycle an old toothbrush.

Once the bristles are worn, clean the toothbrush well and keep it in a handy spot in the kitchen to clean bits of garlic from a press. A toothbrush can be used to clean tight or hard-to-reach spots in other kitchen utensils.

Number 183

Garlic | MINCING GARLIC TO A PASTE

Here's how to produce very fine, smooth bits of garlic without a garlic press. If possible, use kosher or coarse salt; the larger crystals do a better job of breaking down the garlic than fine table salt.

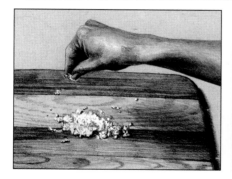

1. Mince the garlic as you normally would on a cutting board. Sprinkle the minced garlic with salt.

2. Drag the side of the chef's knife over the garlic-salt mixture to form a fine puree. Continue to mince and drag the knife as necessary until the puree is smooth.

Number 184

Garlic | MAKING A SMALL AMOUNT OF GARLIC PUREE

The method outlined in tip 183 (page 123) works best with several cloves of garlic. If you just need a dab of pureed garlic for a vinaigrette, try this handy technique.

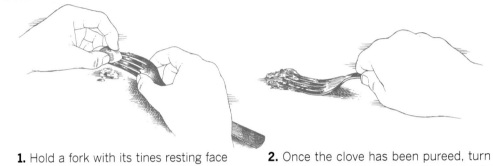

1. Hold a fork with its tines resting face down just above a cutting board. Rub a peeled clove of garlic rapidly back and forth against the tines, close to their points.

2. Once the clove has been pureed, turn the fork over and mash any large chunks to make a smooth puree.

Number 185

Garlic | PUREEING HEADS OF ROASTED GARLIC

Heads of garlic can be drizzled with oil, wrapped in foil, and then roasted in the oven until the garlic is soft and creamy. This technique is simple, but getting the garlic out of the skins is not. Removing excess layers of papery skin before cooking helps. But most sources suggest squeezing the roasted garlic, one clove at a time. Here's how to speed up the process.

1. Cut about 1/4 inch from the tip end of the head of roasted garlic. Place the garlic, cut side down, in a potato ricer.

2. Press down to push the garlic through the ricer. The extruded garlic is nicely pureed, while the peel remains inside the ricer.

Number 186

Ginger | PEELING

Because of its shape, ginger can be difficult to peel, especially if using a knife. Try this method to reduce waste.

Use the bowl of a teaspoon to scrape off the knotty skin from a knob of ginger. The spoon moves easily around curves in the ginger, so you remove just the skin.

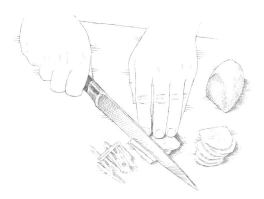

Number 187

Ginger | MINCING

Ginger is highly fibrous, which makes it tricky to mince. A sharp knife is a must. This technique works best.

1. Slice the peeled knob of ginger into thin rounds, then fan the rounds out and cut them into thin matchstick-like strips.

2. Chop the matchsticks crosswise into a fine mince.

Number 188

Ginger | GRATING

Most cooks who use fresh ginger have scraped their fingers on the grater when the piece of ginger gets down to a tiny nub. Instead of cutting a small chunk of ginger off a larger piece and then grating it, try this method.

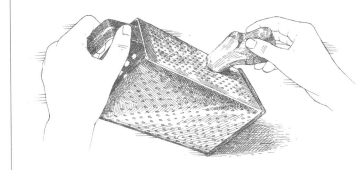

Peel a small section of the large piece of ginger. Grate the peeled portion, using the rest of the ginger as a handle to keep fingers safely away from the grater.

Number 189

Ginger | JUICING

To produce large amounts of ginger juice for dressings or sauces, you must wrap grated ginger in cheesecloth and squeeze. If you need just a teaspoon or two of ginger juice, try this method.

1. Cut off a small piece of peeled ginger from a large knob. Place the piece, about the size of a large garlic clove, into a garlic press.

2. Press down on the ginger. The flesh will stay in the garlic press, while the juice falls through the holes and into a bowl below.

Number 190

Goose | RENDERING THE FAT

A goose has a thick layer of fat right under the skin that must be rendered in the oven. If the fat remains, the skin will be flabby and the meat greasy. This technique can be used with duck, too.

1. With a trussing needle or skewer, prick the goose skin all over, especially around the breast and thighs. Hold the needle nearly parallel to the bird to avoid pricking the meat. These holes provide an exit route for rendered fat.

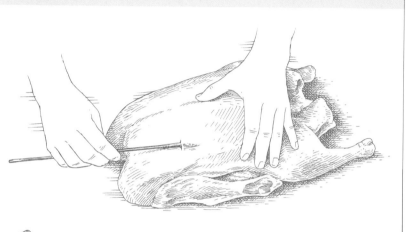

2. Using rubber gloves to protect your hands from possible splashes of boiling water, lower the goose, neck-end down, into a stock pot filled with simmering water, submerging as much of the goose as possible until "goose bumps" appear, about 1 minute. Repeat this process, submerging the goose tail-end down. Dry the goose with paper towels, and then set it on a rack in a roasting pan and refrigerate for 1 to 2 days. The boiling and drying process tightens the skin so that during roasting the fat is squeezed out.

Number 191

Greens |
SEPARATING LEAVES FROM STEMS

Many leafy greens, including Swiss chard, kale, mustard greens, and collards, have thick stems that must either be discarded or cooked separately from the leaves (which is possible with chard). Here's a simple way to slice the leaves away from the thick central stalks.

Hold each leaf at the base of the stem over a bowl filled with water, and use a sharp knife to slash the leafy portion from either side of the thick stem. The cutting motion here is the same that you would use with a machete.

Number 192

Greens | DRYING BLANCHED GREENS

Many leafy greens, such as spinach and kale, benefit from quick cooking in boiling water (a process called blanching) before being sautéed with flavorings. After blanching, it's important to squeeze as much water as possible out of the greens before adding them to the pan. Instead of squeezing the greens by hand, try this method or the one that follows.

1. Place the wet greens in the hopper of a potato ricer.

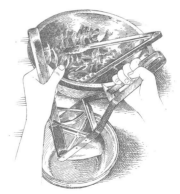

2. Close the handle and squeeze the water from the greens. Don't squeeze more than is necessary, or you might puree the greens.

Number 193

Greens | DRYING BLANCHED GREENS

If you don't own a potato ricer, try this method.

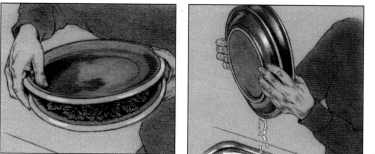

1. Place the blanched greens on a dinner plate and put a second plate on top of them.

2. Squeeze the plates together over the sink until the greens are dry.

Number 194

Grilling: *Gas* | CHECKING GAS LEVEL IN TANK

There's nothing worse than running out of fuel halfway through grilling. If your grill doesn't have a gas gauge, use this technique to estimate how much gas is left in the tank.

1. Bring a cup or so of water to a boil in a small saucepan or glass measuring cup (if using the microwave). Pour the water over the side of the tank.

2. Feel the metal with your hand. Where the water has succeeded in warming the tank, it is empty; where the tank remains cool to the touch, there is still propane inside.

Number 195

Grilling: *Charcoal* | MEASURING VOLUME FOR GRILLING

Many recipes call for a particular volume of charcoal, such as four quarts. Here's an easy way to handle this task.

Open the top of an empty half-gallon carton of milk or juice and wash the carton thoroughly. Store this carton with the charcoal and use it to measure out charcoal. Each full carton equals roughly two quarts.

Number 196

Grilling: *Charcoal* | LIGHTING THE FIRE

Our favorite tool for lighting a charcoal fire is called a chimney, or flue, starter. A chimney starter is shaped like a can, with both ends open. A wood handle on the side helps you move the can around the grill. Inside, a metal plate divides the lower portion (used to hold crumpled newspaper) from the upper portion (where the charcoal rests).

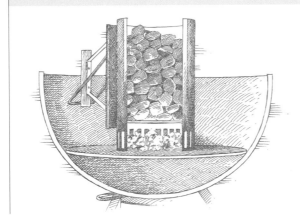

To use a chimney starter, place two or three crumpled sheets of newspaper in the bottom section. Set the starter on the bottom grate in a kettle grill and fill the main compartment with as much charcoal as directed in individual recipes. When you light the newspaper, the flames will shoot up through the charcoal and ignite it. When the coals are covered with light gray ash, they are ready. Simply dump the coals onto the grate and arrange as necessary, using long-handled tongs.

Number 197

Grilling: *Charcoal* | MAKING YOUR OWN CHIMNEY STARTER

Although a chimney starter is relatively inexpensive (about $15 to $20), you may want to save money and improvise with an empty 39-ounce coffee can that has had both ends removed with a can opener. Note that there are two drawbacks to this method. The improvised starter has no handles so you must maneuver it with long-handled tongs. Also, because of its size, this improvised starter can't light enough charcoal for most grilling jobs; you will need to add unlit coals once the lit coals have been dumped onto the charcoal grate.

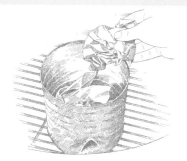

1. Using a church-key can opener, punch six holes along the lower circumference of the can.

2. Set the can on the grill's charcoal rack with the triangular holes at the bottom. Load the can about one-half to two-thirds full with crumpled newspaper, and top it off with charcoal.

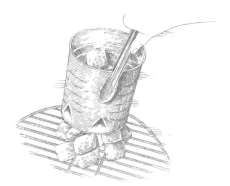

3. Insert a long match through one of the triangular holes at the bottom to set the crumpled paper on fire.

4. When the coals are lit (after about 20 minutes), use tongs to grasp the top of the starter and dump its contents onto the charcoal rack. Place more coals loosely around and on top of the burning coals to build up a cooking fire.

Number 198

Grilling: *Charcoal* | LIGHTING A FIRE WITHOUT A CHIMNEY STARTER

Our preferred method for lighting charcoal calls for a chimney starter (see tips 196 and 197, pages 130–131.). If you don't have a starter, you can use the same principle to the light the coals.

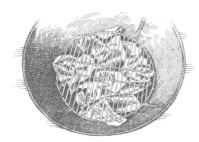

1. Place eight crumpled sheets of newspaper beneath the rack on which the charcoal sits.

2. With the bottom air vents open, pile the charcoal on the rack and light the paper. After about 20 minutes, the coals should be covered with light gray ash and ready for cooking.

Number 199

Grilling: *Charcoal* | BUILDING A TWO-LEVEL FIRE

In many cases, we like to grill over a two-level fire. With this arrangement one part of the grill is very hot, while the other side is cooler. This setup works well for chops and chicken parts, which can be seared on the hot part of the grill and then cooked through more slowly on the cool part of the grill without causing the exterior to char. Having a cool section of the grill also gives the cook a place to drag foods if flames engulf the hot section of the grill.

To build a two-level fire, pile the lit charcoal over half the grill and leave the other half free of coals. Use long-handled tongs to move briquettes into place as necessary.

Number 200

Grilling: *Wood Chips* | MAKING A FOIL PACKET FOR CHIPS

Hickory, mesquite, and other wood chips can be added to a charcoal fire to flavor foods. Here's the best way to keep the chips burning slowly and thus prolong their smoking time.

1. Soak the chips in a bowl of water for at least one hour to slow down the rate at which they will burn. Drain the chips and place them in the center of an 18-inch square of aluminum foil. Fold in all four sides of the foil to enclose the chips.

2. Turn the foil packet over. Tear about six large holes (each the size of a quarter) through the top of the foil packet with a fork to allow smoke to escape. Place the packet, with the holes facing up, directly on top of a pile of lit charcoal.

Number 201

Grilling | CLEANING THE COOKING GRATE

Once coals have been lit and spread out in the bottom of the grill, put the cooking grate in place, and let it heat up for several minutes. Once hot, clean the grill with a wire brush. For foods such as fish, which tend to stick to the grill, take this extra precaution, which also works on a gas grill.

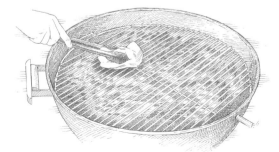

Dip a large wad of paper towels in vegetable oil, grab the wad with tongs, and wipe the grid thoroughly to lubricate it and prevent sticking. This extra step also removes any remaining residue on the grate, which might mar the delicate flavor of fish.

Number 202

Grilling | MEASURING THE HEAT LEVEL

Before cooking, use this technique to determine how hot your fire is. While steaks require a blazing hot fire, vegetables and delicate seafood are best cooked over cooler coals.

Hold your outstretched hand five inches above the cooking grate and count how many seconds you can comfortably leave it in place. When the fire is hot, you won't be able to leave your hand there for more than two seconds. When the fire is medium, you will be able to leave your hand over the grill for four or five seconds. When the fire is medium-low, you will be able to leave your hand in place for about seven seconds.

Number 203

Grilling | MEASURING THE HEAT LEVEL IN A CLOSED KETTLE

If you are grill-roasting a chicken or barbecuing ribs with the lid on, use this method to gauge the temperature inside the grill. For poultry and small roasts, the temperature should be between 300 and 400 degrees. If slow-cooking brisket, ribs, or thick roasts, keep the temperature between 200 and 300 degrees.

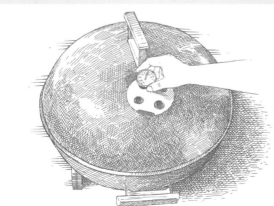

Put the food on the grill and set the lid in place. Open the air vents slightly and insert a grill thermometer (available at most hardware stores) through the vent.

Number 204

Grilling | DOUSING FLAMES WITH A SQUIRT BOTTLE

Nothing's worse than an uncontrolled fire that chars food on the grill. Here's an excellent way to prevent a grease fire from ruining your meal.

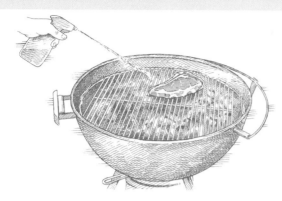

Keep a squirt bottle or plant mister filled with water near the grill. At the first sign of flames, try to pull foods to a cool part of the grill and douse the flames with water.

Number 205

Grilling | ONE PLATTER FOR TWO JOBS

Grilled meat, poultry, and fish should not be returned to the same platter that was used to carry the raw food to the grill. Instead of last-minute fumbling for a new platter, this method uses a single platter for both jobs, which also saves on cleanup time.

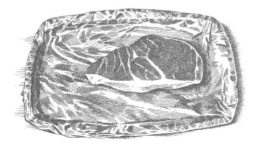
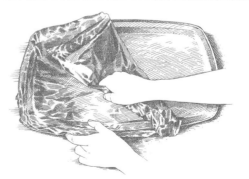

1. Cover the platter with foil before placing the raw food on it.

2. While the food is grilling, remove the foil so you can use the same platter when the food comes off the grill.

135

Number 206

Ground Meat | DEFROSTING EVENLY

A solid hunk of ground meat will start to cook around the edges when defrosted in the microwave. This tip promotes more even defrosting.

With your hands, break the ground meat into chunks and place them in a dish. Cover loosely with plastic wrap and microwave on the defrost setting, rotating pieces of meat if you see any signs that the meat is beginning to cook in spots.

Number 207

Ham | HANDLING A COUNTRY HAM

We love a country ham but find the large size of the ham makes it unwieldy to cook, especially since the ham should be simmered in a stock pot before roasting.

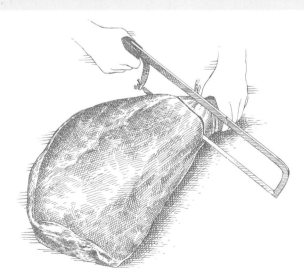

To get around this problem, use a hacksaw to remove the hock end of the ham. The ham should now fit into a large stock pot or roasting pan. Save the hock for cooking beans or greens or making soup.

Number 208

Hash Browns | FLIPPING SAFELY

Hash browns as well as Chinese noodle cakes and Spanish omelets must be browned on both sides in a hot skillet. Most recipes suggest inverting the food onto a plate and then sliding it back into the skillet to cook the second side. We find that the removable bottom from a metal tart pan works better than a plate.

1. Using an oven mitt or potholders, slide the tart pan bottom over the skillet and invert the skillet.

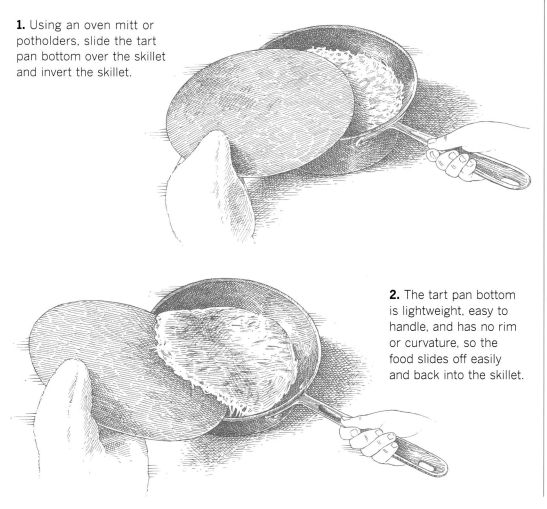

2. The tart pan bottom is lightweight, easy to handle, and has no rim or curvature, so the food slides off easily and back into the skillet.

Number 209

Hazelnuts | TOASTING AND SKINNING

Hazelnuts are covered with a dark brown skin that can be quite bitter. Toasting the nuts in a 350-degree oven until fragrant (about 15 minutes), improves their flavor and also causes the skins to blister and crack so they can be rubbed off.

1. Transfer the toasted nuts to the center of a clean tea towel.

2. Bring up the sides of the towel and twist it closed to seal in the nuts.

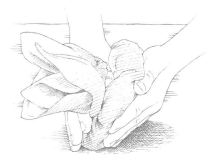

3. Rub the nuts together in the towel to scrape off as much of the brown skin as possible and reveal the light-colored nut-meats. It's fine if patches of skin remain.

4. Carefully open the towel on a flat surface. Gently roll the nuts away from the skins.

Herbs|MAKING A BOUQUET GARNI

A bouquet garni is a classic French combination of herbs and spices used to flavor soups, stocks, and stews. Traditional recipes call for wrapping the herbs and spices in cheesecloth for easy removal before serving. A coffee filter, which most modern cooks are more likely to have on hand, can be used in place of the cheesecloth.

1. Place the herbs (usually bay leaves and thyme, either dried or fresh, and fresh parsley) and spices (usually black peppercorns) into the coffee filter.

2. Tie the end of the coffee filter closed, catching the stems of the herbs as you do so.

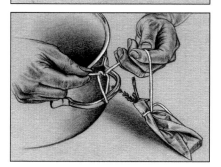

3. Tie the other end of the string to the handle of the pot or pan so you can easily retrieve the bouquet garni once the herbs and spices have given up their flavor.

Number 211

Herbs | RELEASING FLAVOR FROM DRIED HERBS

Flavorful oils in dried oregano, thyme, and other herbs should be released before the herbs are added to foods. You can crush dried herbs between your fingers or use this method for maximum flavor.

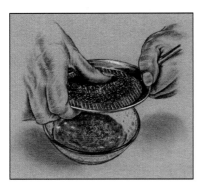

Place the dried herbs in a mesh sieve and push down on them with your fingertips as you shake the sieve back and forth over a bowl. This process not only breaks the leaves into smaller pieces (which incorporate better into soups and stews), it also helps release their flavor.

Number 212

Herbs | KEEPING FRESH

Parsley and other fresh herbs with long stems can be kept for at least a week, if not longer, if you follow this method.

1. Wash and dry the herbs thoroughly. Trim the stem ends, just as you trim the ends of cut flowers.

2. Place the herbs in a tall, airtight container with a tight-fitting lid. Add water up to the top of the stems, but don't cover the leaves. Seal the container tightly and refrigerate. The combination of water and relatively little air keeps the herbs fresher than other storage methods.

Number 213

Ice Cream | LEAKFREE CONES

Children and adults who savor ice cream cones slowly know that the melting ice cream often saturates the tip of the cone, which can result in a messy leak. Here's how to keep the cone dry.

Place a minimarshmallow or upside-down Hershey's Kiss in each cone before loading it up with ice cream, creating a barrier between the melting ice cream and the fragile cone tip.

Number 214

Instant-Read Thermometer | RECALIBRATING

There's no point using an instant-read thermometer if it's not accurate. To test accuracy, insert the probe into a pan of boiling water. The thermometer should register 212 degrees at sea level. (The boiling point drops about one degree for every 500-foot increase in altitude, so compensate accordingly.) If your dial-face thermometer is inaccurate, it can be adjusted.

Turn the thermometer over and use a pair of pliers to adjust the nut beneath the head. This nut controls the position of the gauge. Keep adjusting until the thermometer reads 212 degrees when inserted into boiling water.

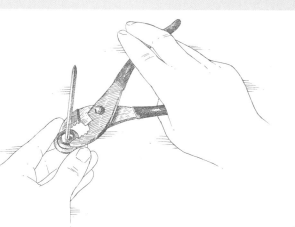

141

Number 215

Instant-Read Thermometer | PROTECTING HANDS FROM POTS

Most instant-read thermometers come with a protective plastic sleeve with a metal clip (for clipping to aprons) that forms a loop at the very top. Use this clip and plastic sleeve to distance your hand from hot pots when taking their temperature.

 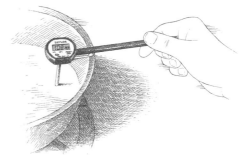

1. Slide the probe end of the thermometer into the loop at the tip of the clip.

2. Hold the end of the plastic sleeve to keep the thermometer upright, and then lower the probe into the hot pot.

Number 216

Instant-Read Thermometer | MEASURING SHALLOW LIQUIDS

Recipes for custards, curds, pastry creams, and other delicate or heat-sensitive mixtures often indicate at what temperature to take them off the heat. If you are cooking a small quantity, use this technique to get an accurate reading with an instant-read thermometer.

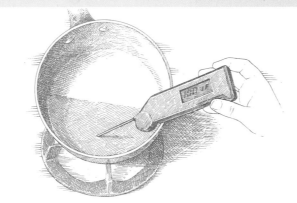

Tilt the pan so that the liquid collects on one side, creating enough depth to get an accurate reading.

Number 217

Jars | USING A RUBBER BAND TO OPEN LIDS

Save those thick rubber bands used to bind bunches of broccoli or keep a lobster claw shut.

Slip the rubber band around the lid of a jar that won't open. The band provides extra grip and should help you open a stuck lid.

Number 218

Kitchen Efficiency | PROTECTING SINKS FROM CRACKS AND CHIPS

With soapy, slippery hands, it's easy to drop a heavy pot or pan into the sink while you're washing it. If you have a porcelain or enameled sink, this can result in an ugly chip or crack.

To protect your sink, lay several wooden spoons in it to cushion the blow in case you drop a heavy pot or pan.

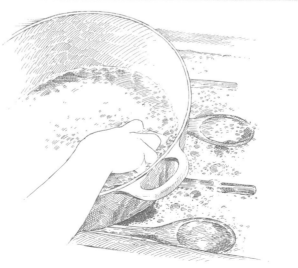

Number 219

Kitchen Efficiency | SECURING THE SILVERWARE TRAY

Most silverware organizers are shorter than the drawers they are placed in. The result is that the organizer and its contents slide to the back of the drawer every time you open it. If you are tired of pulling the organizer forward all the time, here's how to anchor the organizer to the drawer.

1. Affix several small pieces of poster tack, putty, or florist's clay (available at craft stores or flower shops) to the bottom of the organizer.

2. Press the tray into place in the drawer and fill as usual. The organizer will stay put, with no more sliding when you open and shut the drawer.

Number 220

Kitchen Efficiency | HOMEMADE TIERED SHELF

Small items, such as spice jars or extract bottles, can get lost in a well-stocked cabinet. Here's how to keep all items, even those at the back, visible at a glance.

Stack two-by-four pieces of lumber, cut to the right length, to create different height levels within the cabinet. Stack more wood in the back of the cabinet so that items in the rear will be visible above those placed in the front.

Number 221

Kitchen Efficiency | STORING BOXES OF FOIL AND WRAP

The boxes containing plastic sandwich bags, rolls of tin foil, plastic wrap, and the like can use up a lot of valuable drawer space. Here's an efficient way to store these boxes in a cabinet under the counter.

Store the boxes upright in the slots of a cardboard six-pack container that once held beer or soda bottles.

Number 222

Kitchen Efficiency | KEEPING THE REMOTE CONTROL CLEAN

Many cooks enjoy listening to music or watching TV as they cook. But sticky hands can make a real mess out of the remote control.

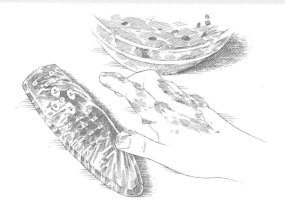

Before cooking, wrap the remote control unit in a layer of clear plastic wrap. The buttons remain visible and operable but don't get smeared by sticky hands.

Number 223

Kitchen Efficiency | KEEPING THE STOVETOP CLEAN

Everyone knows how fat can splatter from a hot skillet. Here's a neat way to sauté and keep the mess under control.

Before you start to cook, lay an overturned cookie sheet or jelly roll pan across the burners next to the pan. The cookie sheet, which is easy to clean, catches most of the grease, leaving the burner plates and stovetop relatively free of fat.

Number 224

Kitchen Efficiency | AN EXTRA-LARGE TRIVET

Many cooks, especially those whose kitchen countertops cannot accommodate hot pots and pans, often have problems finding a spot to put down a hot roasting pan right out of the oven.

To solve this dilemma, we place an overturned jelly roll pan on the counter and use it as a trivet on which to rest a hot roasting pan or Dutch oven.

Number 225

Kitchen Efficiency | CLEANING UP SPILLED OIL

Anyone who has ever dropped a bottle of oil on the floor and had it shatter knows how difficult it can be to clean. Here's how we deal with an oil-slicked floor in our test kitchen.

1. Sprinkle a thick layer of flour over the spilled oil and wait a few minutes for the flour to absorb the oil.

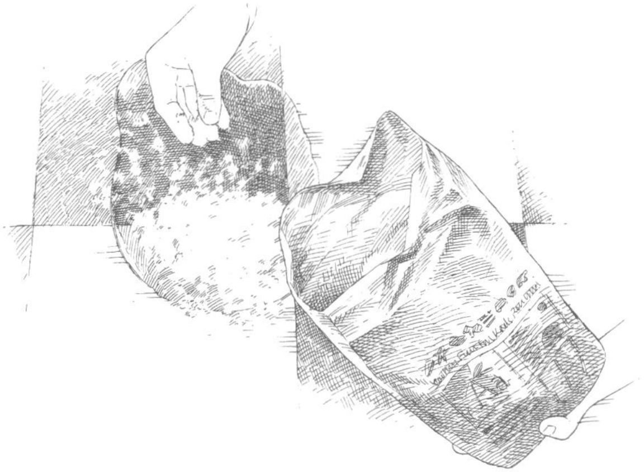

2. With paper towels, or a brush if there is any glass, move the flour around until it absorbs all the oil, then sweep it up with a dustpan and broom.

3. Spray the area with window cleaner and wipe away the last traces of oil and flour.

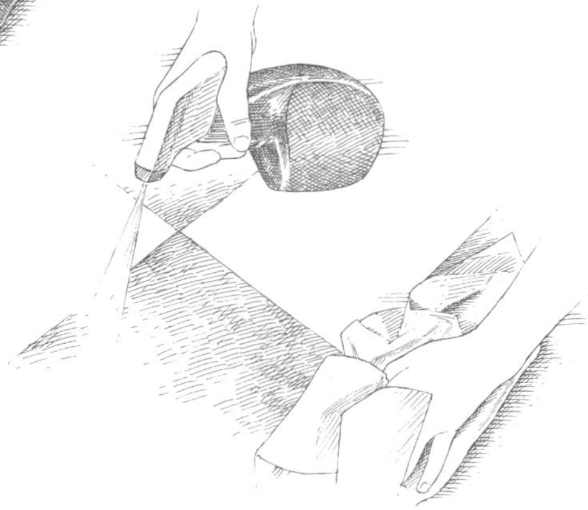

147

Number 226

Kitchen Efficiency | USING A PICTURE FRAME TO HOLD RECIPES

Cooking from recipes scribbled onto note cards or cut from newspapers or magazines can be a chore. Here's how to keep those recipes at eye level and clean.

Slip recipe cards or clipped recipes into a free-standing Lucite picture frame, which slants backward slightly for easier reading and keeps cards free of splatters during cooking.

Number 227

Kiwi | PEELING

A vegetable peeler or knife can have trouble removing the hairy skin from a kiwi fruit. Both tools tend to crush the soft flesh. We like the following method.

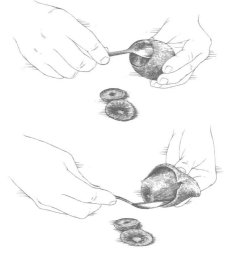

1. Start by trimming the ends of the fruit. Insert a small spoon between the skin and flesh, with the bowl of the spoon facing the flesh. Push the spoon down and carefully move it around the fruit, separating the flesh from the skin.

2. Gently remove the spoon and pull the loosened skin away from the flesh.

Number 228

Lemonade | TWO WAYS TO MASH SLICED LEMONS

We find that sugaring sliced lemons and then mashing them to release their flavorful oils creates the best lemonade ever. Although you can mash the sugared lemons with a potato masher or wooden spoon, here are two ways to work more quickly.

A. Place the sliced lemons and sugar in the bowl of a standing mixer fitted with the paddle attachment. Turn the mixer to low and mix for about 45 seconds. (Longer mixing can actually mash the lemons too much and make the lemonade bitter.) To prevent splatters, drape a kitchen towel over the mixer.

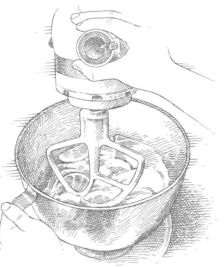

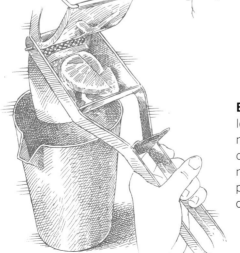

B. An alternative method is to let sugared lemon slices macerate for about 15 minutes, or until softened, and then mash them in batches with a potato ricer. Set the ricer right over the lemonade pitcher.

149

Number 229

Lemons | REMOVING PEEL FROM A GRATER

Lemon zest often becomes trapped in the teeth of a box grater and ends up being wasted. Here are two ways to get around this problem.

A. Cover the grater with a piece of waxed paper before grating. The zest will remain on top of the wax paper rather than clogging the grater's teeth.

B. If you don't have wax paper on hand, use a toothbrush, kept especially for this purpose in the kitchen, to scrape the trapped zest off the grater.

Number 230

Lemons | JUICING

Everyone has a trick for juicing lemons. We find this method extracts the most juice possible from lemons as well as limes.

1. Start by rolling the lemon on a hard surface, pressing down firmly with the palm of your hand to break membranes inside the fruit.

2. Cut the lemon in half. Use a wooden reamer to extract the juice into a bowl. To catch the seeds, place a mesh strainer over the bowl.

Number 231

Lemons | FREEZING SPENT SHELLS

Here's a nifty use for the spent shells from juiced lemons and limes.

Place spent shells in a zipper-lock bag in the freezer. When you need acidulated water to hold peeled apples, potatoes, or artichokes, don't waste a fresh lemon—just take a spent shell from the freezer. It has enough juice and acidity to keep these foods from turning brown.

Number 232

Lettuce | CORING AND WASHING

Here's a simple way to core and wash a head of iceberg lettuce with just one motion.

 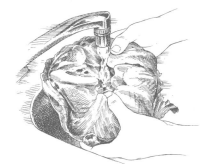

1. Rap the bottom of the head of lettuce sharply on the counter to loosen the core. Turn the head of lettuce over and pull out the core in one piece.

2. Fill the hole left by the extracted core with water to rinse soil from the lettuce. Separate the leaves, wash again if necessary, and dry.

Number 233

Lobsters | DISTINGUISHING HARD SHELLS FROM SOFT SHELLS

Right after molting, a lobster has a soft shell that is easy to crack. However, hard-shelled lobsters are much meatier. Here's how to tell the difference between the two stages in the lobster's life cycle.

Squeeze the side of the lobster's body, just in front of the tail. A soft-shell lobster will yield to pressure, while a hard-shell lobster will feel hard and tightly packed with meat.

Number 234

Mangoes | PEELING

Mangoes are notoriously hard to peel, owing to their odd shape and slippery texture. Here's how we handle this tough kitchen task. This method ensures long, attractive strips of fruit.

1. Start by removing a thin slice from one end of the mango so that it sits flat on a work surface.

2. Hold the mango cut side down and remove the skin with a sharp paring knife in thin strips, working from top to bottom.

3. Once the peel has been removed, cut down along the side of the flat pit to remove the flesh from one side of the mango. Do the same thing on the other side of the pit.

4. Trim around the pit to remove any remaining flesh. The flesh can now be chopped or sliced as desired.

Number 235

Mayonnaise | DRIZZLING IN THE OIL

Homemade mayonnaise is made by slowly whisking oil into beaten egg yolk and lemon juice. It can be difficult to whisk with one hand and hold a heavy measuring cup and pour evenly with the other hand.

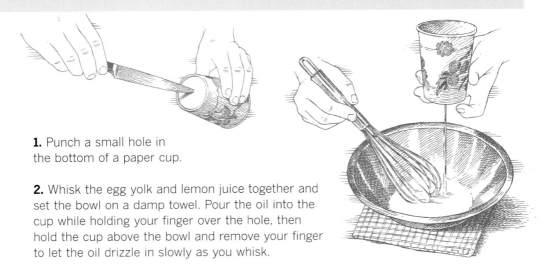

1. Punch a small hole in the bottom of a paper cup.

2. Whisk the egg yolk and lemon juice together and set the bowl on a damp towel. Pour the oil into the cup while holding your finger over the hole, then hold the cup above the bowl and remove your finger to let the oil drizzle in slowly as you whisk.

Number 236

Meat | SPACING TIES ON A ROAST

Roasts cook more evenly when tied at even intervals. Tying also makes the roast more attractive to serve. Here's an easy way to ensure you have evenly spaced the pieces of kitchen twine.

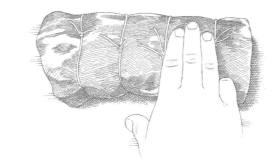

Space the ties about three fingers apart down the entire length of the roast.

Number 237

Meat | FREEZING FOR EASY SLICING

Many recipes, including stir-fries, soups, and pasta sauces, call for thinly sliced pieces of flank steak, pork tenderloin, or other meats. Here's how to make the slices as thin as possible.

Place the meat in the freezer until partially frozen, 1 to 2 hours depending on the thickness of the meat. It's much easier to slice through partially frozen meat and turn out thin, even slices.

Number 238

Meatballs | ENSURING EVEN BROWNING

Meatballs must be cooked through and taste best when browned evenly on all sides. Their round shape can make this a challenge.

Once the meatballs have been browned on their two broader sides, use tongs to stand them on their sides to finish cooking. If necessary, lean the meatballs up against each other to get the final sides browned.

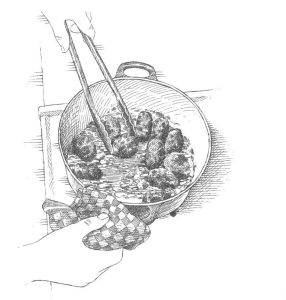

Number 239

Meatloaf | HELPING FAT DRAIN OFF

No one wants a greasy meatloaf. Unfortunately, this is just what you get when you bake meatloaf in a standard loaf pan.

1. We prefer to use a loaf pan with a perforated insert. The rendered fat falls into the bottom pan, away from the meat.

2. To help ensure that the fat falls away, use a fork to pull the ground meat mixture away from the sides of the pan before baking.

Number 240

Milk | PREVENTING BOILOVERS

Milk has a tendency to foam up and eventually boil over when being heated in a pan.

1. Before pouring the milk into the pan, rub butter along the top edge and inside the lip of the pan.

2. Add the milk and bring to a simmer. Even if the milk does foam up, it will stop when it hits the butter.

Number 241

Mixers: *Handheld* | KEEPING BOWLS IN PLACE

Many recipes call for adding wet and dry ingredients alternately for even blending. Here's how to secure the bowl so you can hold a mixer in one hand and add ingredients with the other.

1. Twist a damp towel to form a turban nest slightly larger than the base of the bowl.

2. Set the bowl into the turban nest, which will hold the bowl in place as you mix and add ingredients.

Number 242

Mixers: *Standing* | MOVING HEAVY MIXERS

Many standing mixers, as well as food processors, are heavy and don't slide easily. They can be difficult for many people to lift. Here's a good way to move them around the counter with ease.

Place your mixer on a towel or cloth place mat that can be pulled anywhere on the counter with little effort.

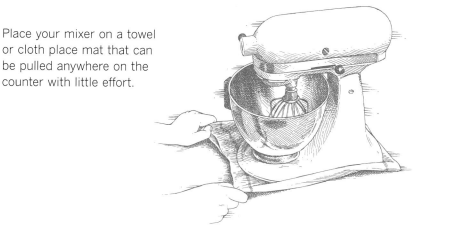

Number 243

Mixers: *Standing* | KEEPING THE MESS UNDER CONTROL

Dry ingredients can puff out in a cloud of fine particles when mixed, while wet ingredients, such as cream or liquidy batters, can cause splatters. Here's a good way to keep your counter clean when using a standing mixer.

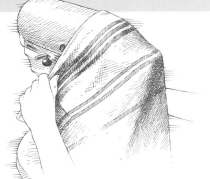

Once the ingredients are in the bowl, drape a clean, very damp dish towel over the front of the mixer and bowl. Draw the towel snug with one hand and then turn on the mixer. When done, simply wash the towel.

Number 244

Mortar and Pestle | IMPROVISING WITH A COFFEE MUG

Stone, marble, wood, or porcelain mortars (bowls) and pestles (dowel-shaped grinding tools) are great for grinding chiles, spices, nuts, or even herbs. Many modern kitchens are not equipped with this tool. Here's how to make a mortar and pestle with objects likely to be found in any kitchen.

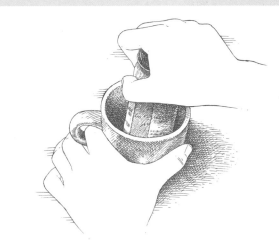

Place the ingredients to be ground in a shallow, diner-style stoneware coffee cup (which will be the mortar) and use a heavy glass spice bottle as the pestle.

Number 245

Mushrooms | FLAVORING PORTOBELLOS

Big, meaty portobello caps can be studded with garlic and herbs, just like a piece of meat.

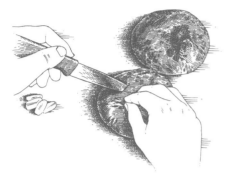

1. Use the tip of a paring knife to make 10 or 12 narrow slits in the top of each portobello cap.

2. Insert a sliver of garlic into each slit along with a sage leaf, some fresh rosemary, or maybe a tiny sprig of thyme. The garlic and herbs will remain inside the portobello as it cooks.

Number 246

Mushrooms | SLICING BUTTONS QUICKLY

Slicing button mushrooms thinly takes some patience. Here's a novel way to speed up the process.

Trim a thin piece from the stem end of each mushroom, then cut the trimmed mushrooms, one at a time, in an egg slicer. The pieces will be even and thin.

Number 247

Mushrooms | SOAKING DRIED PORCINI

Dried porcini, as well as shiitakes, oysters, and other dried mushrooms, must be reconstituted before being added to recipes. Soak the porcini in hot tap water (about 1 cup per ounce of dried mushrooms) in a small bowl until softened, about 20 minutes. Here's how to make sure any sand or dirt released by the mushrooms doesn't end up in your food.

1. Most of the sand and dirt will fall to the bottom of the bowl, so use a fork to lift the rehydrated mushrooms from the liquid without stirring up the sand.

2. Never discard the flavorful soaking liquid, which can be added to soups, sauces, rice dishes, or pasta sauces. To remove the grit, pour the liquid through a small sieve lined with a single sheet of paper towel and placed over a measuring cup.

Number 248

Mussels | DEBEARDING

Mussels often contain a weedy beard protruding from the crack between the two shells. It's fairly small and can be difficult to tug out of place. Here's how we handle this task.

Trap the beard between the side of a small knife and your thumb and pull to remove it. The flat surface of the paring knife gives you some leverage to extract this pesky beard.

Number 249

Nuts | CHOPPING QUICKLY

Chopping a large batch of nuts can be a tedious task. Here's how to speed up the process.

Place the nuts on a cutting board and hold two chef's knives parallel to each other in one hand and chop. Use the other hand to guide the knives through the nuts.

Number 250

Oatmeal | TOASTING

We have discovered that the secret to great-tasting oatmeal with a rich nutty flavor is toasting the oatmeal in butter before adding the milk or water. This tip works with steel-cut or rolled oats.

Melt a tablespoon or so of butter per cup of oats that will be cooked in a skillet. When the butter just begins to foam, add the oats and toast, stirring constantly with a wooden spoon, until golden and fragrant, with a butterscotch-like aroma, 1½ to 2 minutes. Stir the oats into simmering water and/or milk and cook as you normally would.

Number 251

Oil | POURING SMOOTHLY

Many households buy olive oil in gallon containers, pouring some into a smaller can or bottle for daily use. But pouring from such a huge container can be a problem, especially when the oil glugs and sloshes out.

1. To even out the flow while pouring, use a can opener to punch a hole in the top of the container opposite the pouring spout.

2. Having thus evened out the pressure in the container, the oil will pour in a smooth, continuous flow.

Number 252

Onions | STORING VIDALIAS

The sugar content of Vidalia onions, which is what endears them to many cooks, also makes them spoil more quickly if they are stored touching each other. The same thing holds true for other sweet onions such as Walla Wallas and Mauis. Here's how to prolong their freshness.

Place one onion in the leg of an old but clean pair of pantyhose. Tie a knot in the hose, just above the onion. Repeat this process up the entire leg of the pantyhose.

Number 253

Onions | EASIER PEELING

There are many ways to remove the papery skin from the exterior of an onion. We think this is the easiest method.

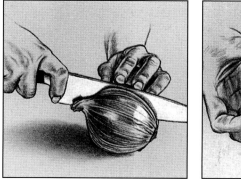
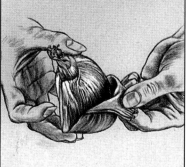

1. Halve the onion lengthwise, cutting from end to end.

2. Grab hold of the skin along the cut edge and simply peel it off the entire onion half.

Number 254

Onions | GRILLING RINGS

Onion slices can be difficult to handle on the grill, with rings often slipping through the grate and onto the coals. Here's how to grill onions safely and easily.

1. Cut thick slices (at least ½ inch) from large red, Vidalia, or Spanish onions and impale them all the way through with a slender bamboo skewer (should be about the same thickness as a toothpick or a thin metal skewer). If using longer skewers, thread two slices on each skewer.

2. The skewered onion slices remain intact as they grill so no layers can fall onto the coals. Best of all, the onions are easily flipped with tongs.

Number 255

Orange Juice | SHORTCUTTING FROZEN JUICE PREPARATION

When the craving for orange juice hits, waiting for a can of frozen concentrate to thaw before mixing it with water can be frustrating. Here's a way to avoid the wait.

1. Run the can of frozen concentrate under hot water so it will melt just enough to release from the can.

2. Use an immersion blender to mix the still-frozen block of concentrate with water. The action of the blender produces a smooth, lumpfree juice—with no waiting.

Number 256

Oranges | REMOVING SEGMENTS

For salads and other dishes where presentation matters, you will want to remove segments from an orange without any white pith or membranes. Here's how. Use the same technique with grapefruit.

1. Start by slicing a small section, about ¹/₂ inch thick, off the top and bottom ends of the fruit.

2. With the fruit resting flat on a work surface, use a very sharp paring knife to slice off the rind, including all of the bitter white pith. Slide the knife edge from the top to the bottom of the fruit, following the outline of the fruit as closely as possible to minimize waste.

3. Working over a bowl to catch the juice, slip the blade between a membrane and one section of fruit and slice to the center, separating one side of the section.

4. Turn the blade of the knife so that it is facing out and is lined up along the membrane on the opposite side of the section. Slide the blade from the center out along the membrane to completely free the section. Continue until all the sections are removed and free of the membranes.

Number 257

Oysters | SHUCKING

An oyster knife with a slightly angled, pointed tip is the best tool for opening oysters. The long blade can also be used to detach the oyster meat from the shell.

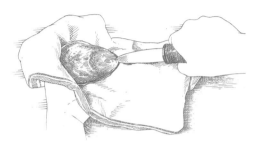

1. Start by holding the oyster cupped-side down in a kitchen towel. (The towel is essential because it will protect your hand in case the knife slips.) Make sure to keep the oyster flat as you work, to keep the flavorful juices from spilling out of the shell. With the tip of the knife, locate the hinge that connects the top and bottom shells.

2. Push between the edges of the shells, wiggling back and forth to pry them open.

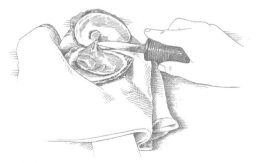

3. Detach the meat from the top shell and discard the shell.

4. To make eating easier, sever the muscle that holds the oyster meat to the bottom shell. The oyster is ready to be served.

Number 258

Pan Drippings | SEPARATING FAT FROM DRIPPINGS

Once a roast comes out of the oven, the bottom of the pan is covered with flavorful pan drippings, which can be used to make a delicious gravy or sauce. However, if the bird or meat has rendered a lot of fat, some of that fat must be removed or the sauce or gravy will be greasy. This laboratory trick works at home.

Pour all the liquid from the roasting pan into a glass measuring cup. The amber pan drippings will fall to the bottom, and the clear fat will rise to the top. Carefully slip a transparent bulb baster beneath the fat layer and pull the pan juices into the baster. Squeeze the pan juices into a saucepan and repeat until only fat remains in the measuring cup. Don't worry if a little fat ends up in the saucepan. As long as you remove most of the fat, the sauce won't be greasy.

Number 259

Pancakes | KEEPING THEM WARM

Pancakes are best eaten as soon as they come off the griddle. Of course, this isn't always possible. Here's how to keep them warm for a few minutes while you round up the troops.

Place the pancakes on a platter lined with a clean cloth napkin or tea towel. Pull the towel over the pancakes and then cover with an inverted colander to keep them warm.

Number 260

Parchment Paper | STORING BULK PAPER

Parchment paper is a must for many baking projects. To save money, we like to buy it in bulk in sheets (rather than rolls), but storing a large quantity can be a challenge. Here's how to keep parchment safe and out of the way.

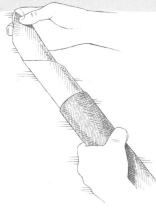

Roll a quantity of parchment paper sheets into a tight roll and slide the roll inside an empty gift-wrap tube, which can be easily stored in the pantry or kitchen. The sheets can be pulled out easily, one at a time.

Number 261

Pasta | HEATING THE SERVING BOWL

If you are serving pasta in a large bowl, it should be heated so the pasta doesn't cool off. If you have forgotten to heat the bowl in a 200-degree oven, here's a last-minute method that works just fine.

Place a colander in the serving bowl and pour the pasta and cooking water into the colander. Lift up the colander and let the hot cooking water stand in the bowl for several seconds to heat it up. Drain the bowl (there's no need to dry it), and then toss the pasta and sauce in the hot bowl.

Number 262

Pastry Bag | FILLING THE BAG

A pastry bag is a must for decorating a cake and many other baking jobs. Getting the frosting (or the filling for deviled eggs) into the bag can be messy. You certainly don't want the frosting to end up on the exterior of the bag, which can happen if you're not careful. Here are two ways to prevent that from occurring.

A. Roll the top of the bag down about 2 inches and use an ice cream scoop to pack the frosting into the bag.

B. If you don't have an ice cream scoop, try rolling down the top of the bag and then fitting it into a Pilsner beer glass. Fold the cuff at the top of the bag over the top of the glass, and spoon the frosting down into the bottom of the bag, which is held snugly in the glass.

Number 263

Pastry Bag | MESS-FREE PIPING

Sometimes you want to use the same pastry bag to pipe two different fillings or frostings. Instead of washing the bag and then waiting for it to dry, try this method. We often use this technique even when using just one filling; it saves on clean-up time.

1. Place the filling or frosting in a large plastic bag.

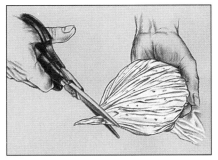

2. Twist the top end of the bag closed and snip a small hole in the bottom.

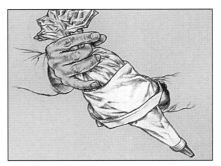

3. Place the filled plastic bag, trimmed end first, into a pastry bag fitted with the desired tip.

4. Pipe until you have used up all the filling or frosting. When done, simply throw out the shriveled bag. The pastry bag is clean and can be put away or loaded with another filled plastic bag.

Number 264

Pastry Cream | QUICK COOLING

Pastry cream and puddings come off the stove hot but must be cooled to room temperature, or even chilled, before they can be used. By maximizing the surface area from which steam can escape, you will speed up the process.

1. Spread the pastry cream or pudding out across a rimmed baking pan that has been covered with plastic wrap.

2. Once the pastry cream or pudding has been spread to the edges of the pan, cover it with another piece of wrap to keep a skin from forming. Snip a number of holes in the plastic wrap to allow steam to escape.

Number 265

Peaches | REMOVING THE PIT

If you're tired of wrestling with peaches and nectarines to remove the pit, try this method, in which the peach splits neatly so the pit can be removed.

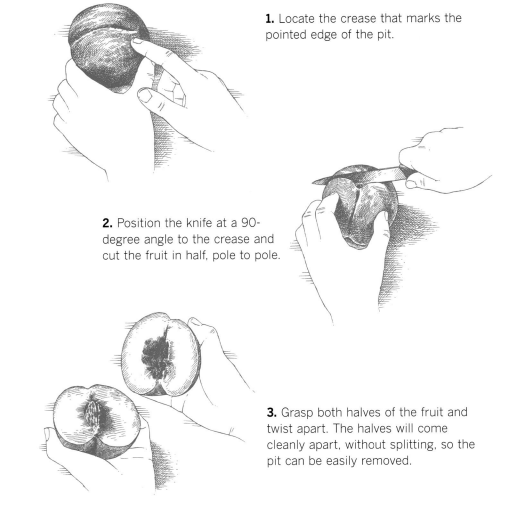

1. Locate the crease that marks the pointed edge of the pit.

2. Position the knife at a 90-degree angle to the crease and cut the fruit in half, pole to pole.

3. Grasp both halves of the fruit and twist apart. The halves will come cleanly apart, without splitting, so the pit can be easily removed.

Number 266

Peaches | PEELING

Some recipes, especially for pies, call for peeled peaches. A vegetable peeler often mashes the fruit, while a knife trims a lot of edible flesh with the skin. Use this method instead, which also works with nectarines.

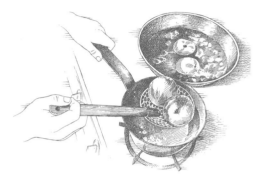 

1. Bring a small saucepan of water to a boil. Add the peaches and simmer, turning once or twice, for 30 seconds. Use a slotted spoon or mesh skimmer to transfer the peaches to a bowl of ice water to stop the cooking process.

2. When cool enough to handle, remove the peaches from the water and slip the skins off with your fingers.

Number 267

Peanut Butter | BLENDING NATURAL BUTTERS

Fans of natural peanut butter (without sugar or other stabilizers), tahini, and other nut butters know that the butter often separates into a dense, solid mass beneath a layer of oil that has risen to the surface. Before spreading, the oil and the solids have to be reblended. A spoon just makes a mess of everything. Try this trick instead.

Turn the sealed jar upside down and allow the oil to rise again to the top. As the oil passes through the nut butter, the solids will absorb some oil and become soft enough to spread. Flip the jar right-side up, and the peanut butter is ready to use.

Number 268

Pears | CORING

We find that a pear really should be cut in half to get at the core.

1. Use a melon baller to cut around the central core with a circular motion.

2. Draw the melon baller from the central core to the top of the pear, removing the interior portion of the stem as you go.

3. Use the melon baller to remove the blossom end as well.

Number 269

Pepper Mill | KEEPING THE GRINDER CLEAN

Preparing raw cutlets, ground meat, or poultry for cooking can leave the cook's hands greasy and slippery when it is time to season the meat. Here's how to grind fresh pepper over meats, even when your hands are dirty.

Before you handle the meat, drape a small piece of plastic wrap over the pepper mill. Your hands only touch the plastic, which can be removed and discarded once the meat has been seasoned.

Number 270

Pepper Mill | PREVENTING A PEPPERY MESS

Cooks who use a mill to grind their own pepper know that even the best mill invariably leaves a mess of ground pepper on the surface where it is set down. Here's how to avoid this nuisance and capture every last bit of pepper from your grinder.

When you're done using the mill, set it in a small ceramic dish, such as a ramekin or Japanese soy sauce dish. Excess pepper ends up in the dish, not on the counter, and can even be collected, measured, and used in your cooking.

175

Number 271

Peppers | ROASTING

Most recipes instruct the cook to roast whole peppers under the broiler until blackened. The uneven shape of a bell pepper means that one part always burns while another remains undercooked. We prefer to flatten the peppers before roasting, which means that they cook evenly and are much easier to peel. As an added bonus, the seeds can be removed before roasting, not after, when your hands are slippery and the seeds stick to everything.

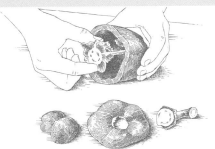

1. Start by removing a ¼-inch-thick slice from the top and bottom of each pepper. Remove the stem from the top lobe. Reach into the pepper and pull out the seeds in a single bunch.

2. Slit down one side of the pepper, then lay it flat, skin side down. Slide a sharp knife along the inside of the pepper to remove all the white ribs and any remaining seeds.

3. Arrange the flattened peppers and the top and bottom pieces, all skin-side up, on a baking sheet lined with foil. Flatten the strips with the palm of your hand.

4. Roast the peppers under the broiler until the skins are charred but the flesh is still firm. Wrap the pan tightly with foil and steam the peppers to help loosen the skins. When the peppers are cool enough to handle, peel off the skin in large strips.

Number 272

Pies: *Crumb Crusts* | PRESSING CRUMBS INTO PLACE

Pressing graham cracker crumbs into a pie plate can be a messy proposition, especially when the buttered and sugared crumbs stick to your hands.

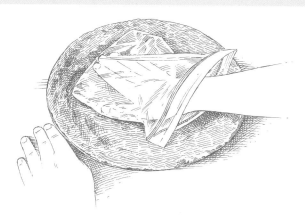

Keep the crumbs where they belong by sheathing your hand in a plastic sandwich bag and pressing the crumbs firmly but neatly.

Number 273

Pies: *Crumb Crusts* | LOOSENING THE CRUST FOR EASY SLICING

Because they tend to stick to the pie plate, crumb crusts can be tricky to slice. Here's how we loosen the crust to ensure neat slices.

Fill a large bowl with warm water and dip the bottom of the pie plate into the water for several seconds. The gentle heat should loosen the crust so slices can be cut and removed easily.

Number 274

Pies: *Dough* | ADDING ICE WATER

Most pie pastry recipes use ice water to bring the dough together. However, if you add too much water, the dough can become mushy. Instead of sprinkling water, one tablespoon at a time, over the dough, try this method.

Fill a small spray bottle with the recommended amount of water and spray evenly over the flour mixture to moisten it. Start mixing the dough, spraying with more water as needed, until the dough holds together when pinched. This method ensures that the water is evenly distributed over the flour mixture, making it unlikely that you will add too much water.

Number 275

Pies: *Dough* | MAKESHIFT ROLLING PIN

We find that a tapered wooden pin does the best job of rolling out pie pastry. However, rented vacation condos and cottages often have poorly equipped kitchens. Here's a neat trick for rolling out dough when a pin is nowhere to be found.

An unopened wine bottle with smooth sides has the right weight and shape for rolling out dough. If possible, use white wine and chill the bottle. The cold temperature of the bottle will help keep the butter in the dough chilled.

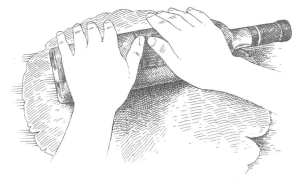

Number 276

Pies: *Dough* | PREVENTING STICKING

It seems that no matter how much you flour the counter, pie dough often sticks as you roll it out. Adding more flour isn't the solution and can actually make the dough tough.

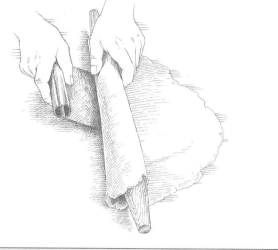

Instead, slide a bench scraper (also called a dough scraper) under the dough every 30 seconds or so. This way the dough never has a chance to stick, and it won't tear when you need to move it. If you don't own a bench scraper, use a metal spatula in the same fashion.

Number 277

Pies: *Dough* | MEASURING THE DOUGH

There's nothing worse than transferring the rolled dough to a pie plate only to realize you haven't rolled it large enough. Here's an easy way to measure the dough as you work.

Invert the pie plate over the dough. There should be an inch or two of extra dough on all sides of the pie plate.

Number 278

Pies: *Dough* | MOVING THE DOUGH

Once the dough has been rolled out evenly, it must be transferred to the pie plate. This is how we like to accomplish this delicate task.

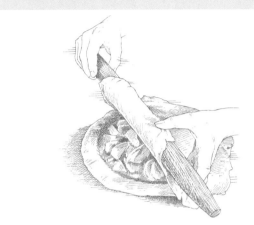

Work a bench scraper or thin spatula under the dough, then roll the dough onto the rolling pin (see tip 276 on page 179). Move the pin over to the pie plate and gently unroll the dough over the filling.

Number 279

Pies: *Dough* | CUTTING AWAY EXTRA DOUGH

Excess dough must be trimmed so that you can fashion a neat edge for the pie.

We find that kitchen shears make the best tool for slicing away extra dough. Leave about ½ inch of dough hanging over the rim of the pie plate so you have something to flute.

Number 280

Pies: *Dough* | FOLDING EXCESS DOUGH UNDER

To create a fluted edge around the exterior of the pie, you need a sturdy, thick piece of dough.

Fold the excess dough back under itself, pressing it firmly to seal. This double-thick edge can be fluted or decorated as desired.

Number 281

Pies: *Dough* | FLUTING THE EDGE

A fluted edge makes the pie especially attractive. It also helps contain the filling.

Hold the inside of the dough with the thumb and forefinger on one hand and press the outside of the dough with the forefinger on the other hand.

Number 282

Pies: *Dough* | PROTECTING THE RIM

The fluted edge on a pie can burn in the oven because it's so exposed. Many recipes suggest piecing together strips of foil to fashion a protective cover for the edge. Instead of trying to twist pieces of foil together, we prefer to use a single sheet to cover the pie edge. Or you can use a disposable aluminum pie plate.

A1. Lay out a square of foil slightly larger than the pie. Fold the square in half and then in half again to form a smaller square. Place the closed corner point in the center of the pie and cut an arc that matches up with the edge of the pie.

A2. When you unfold the foil, you will have cut out a circle from the middle of the sheet. This open circle exposes the filling, while the remaining ring of foil covers the crust.

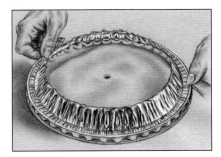

B. A second method for protecting the crust starts with a disposable aluminum pie plate. Cut out the center of the plate and then place the trimmed plate, top-side down, over the rim of the crust.

Number 283

Pies | ADDING CUSTARD FILLINGS

We find that custard fillings, including pumpkin filling, should be poured into the prebaked pie shell when both the custard and pie shell are hot. Here's how to accomplish this task.

Once the pie shell has browned sufficiently, open the oven, pull out the oven rack, and pour the hot custard filling directly into the pie shell.

Number 284

Pies | APPLYING A MERINGUE TOPPING

There's nothing worse than a meringue topping that is uneven or has shrunk back around the edges of the pie. Here's how to get an even meringue topping that covers the entire surface of the pie.

1. Put dabs of meringue over the filling.

2. Once all the meringue has been placed on the pie, use a rubber spatula to "anchor" the meringue to the edge of the crust. As long as the meringue touches the crust, it won't pull away or shrink in the oven.

Number 285

Pineapple | PREPARING

A pineapple can seem daunting to peel and core. We find that the following method is easy and reliable.

1. Start by trimming the ends of the pineapple so it will sit flat on a work surface. Cut the pineapple through the ends into four quarters.

2. Lay each quarter, cut-side up, on a work surface, and slide a knife between the skin and flesh to remove the skin.

3. Stand each peeled quarter on end and slice off the portion of tough, light-colored core attached to the inside of the piece. The peeled and cored pineapple can be sliced as desired.

Number 286

Pine Nuts | TOASTING EVENLY

Pine nuts are difficult to toast evenly on the stovetop. Because of their shape, they tend to rest on one side and are prone to burning.

We find that a hand-cranked stove-top popcorn popper is the perfect vessel for toasting pine nuts. Just heat the popper, add the nuts, and then use the crank to keep the nuts in constant motion until they are evenly toasted.

Number 287

Pizza | KEEPING INTERESTING TOPPINGS ON HAND

Homemade pizza is a blank canvas for the creative use of toppings. The problem is that you don't always have enough topping options on hand. Here's a simple solution to creating interesting pizzas.

Whenever you are cooking something that would make a good pizza topping, reserve a little bit in a clean yogurt or cottage cheese container, label it, and freeze it. When pizza is on the menu, sort through the frozen topping options, defrost what you want in the microwave, and top the pizza creatively.

Number 288

Pizza | GETTING TOPPINGS HOT ON A GRILLED PIE

Grilled pizza is delicious, but often the crust starts to burn on the bottom before the toppings are hot. It's imperative to top grilled pizzas very lightly and use ingredients that will cook quickly. Here's a good way to ensure that the toppings get nice and hot.

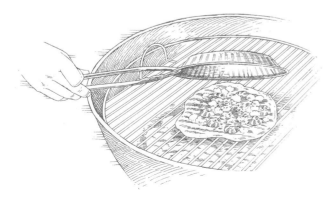

Once the toppings have been applied, invert a disposable aluminum pie plate over the pizza. The pie plate traps heat and creates an ovenlike effect.

Number 289

Pizza | DETERMINING WHEN A DEEP-DISH PIE IS DONE

It can be hard to tell when a deep-dish pizza is done, especially if cheese and toppings are obscuring the crust. Just because the toppings are sizzling doesn't mean the crust is cooked through.

Use a spatula to lift up the pizza slightly. If the bottom crust is nicely browned, the pizza is done.

Number 290

Pizza | CUTTING WITH SCISSORS

When cutting pizza, a regular knife can catch and drag the melted cheese, and pizza wheels often dent the pan when you bear down to cut through the crust.

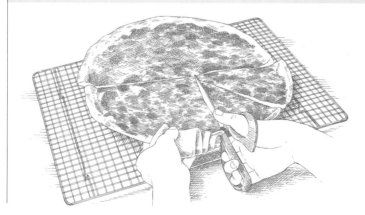

A pair of kitchen shears cuts neatly and easily through pizza. Just hold the edge with a folded paper towel to pick the crust up a bit and make the slicing angle easier.

Number 291

Polenta | SMOOTHING OUT LUMPS

Even if you add the cornmeal to the water in a slow, steady stream, your polenta might have tiny lumps in it. Here's how to get rid of the lumps and produce perfectly smooth polenta.

Once the polenta has finished cooking, use an immersion blender to smooth out any lumps. The blender can also be used to help incorporate butter, cheese, or herbs added just before serving.

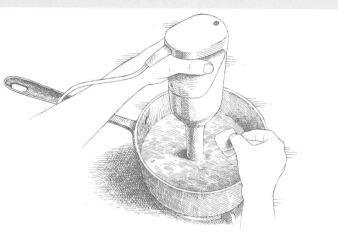

Number 292

Pork Tenderloin | REMOVING THE SILVER SKIN

The tenderloin is covered with a thin, pearlescent membrane, called the silver skin. If left on the meat, the silver skin shrinks and can cause the tenderloin to bow and thus cook unevenly. Here's how to remove the silver skin before cooking the tenderloin.

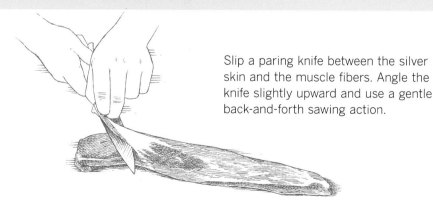

Slip a paring knife between the silver skin and the muscle fibers. Angle the knife slightly upward and use a gentle back-and-forth sawing action.

Number 293

Pork Tenderloin | READYING FOR STIR-FRIES

Our favorite cut of pork for stir-frying is the tenderloin, which is lean and tender. Here's how we get thin, even strips from this long piece of meat.

1. Freeze the tenderloin until firm, 1 to 2 hours. Cut the tenderloin crosswise into ⅓-inch-thick medallions.

2. Slice each medallion into ⅓-inch-wide strips.

Number 294

Potatoes | SCRUBBING CLEAN

Recipes in which the potatoes are not peeled usually instruct the cook to "scrub" the potatoes. This same technique is used with other root vegetables, such as turnips, carrots, beets, or sweet potatoes, that will be cooked with the skin on. Here's a quick and easy way to loosen dirt from the exterior of potatoes and other root vegetables.

Buy a rough-textured "bathing" or "exfoliating" glove especially for use in the kitchen. The glove cleans away dirt but is relatively gentle and won't scrub away the potato skin.

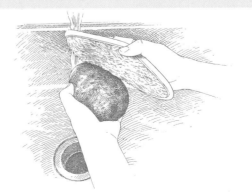

Number 295

Potatoes | OPENING A BAKED POTATO

For the best results, we bake potatoes in a 350-degree oven until tender, about 75 minutes. To ensure that the flesh does not steam and become dense, it's imperative to open up each baked potato as soon as it comes out of the oven. This technique maximizes the amount of steam released and keeps the potato fluffy and light.

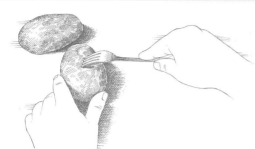 

1. Use the tines of a fork to make a dotted X on top of each potato.

2. Press in at the ends of the potato to push the flesh up and out. Besides releasing steam quickly, this method helps the potato trap and hold onto bits of butter.

Number 296

Potatoes | DRYING GRATED POTATOES

Recipes for potato pancakes, roesti, and hash browns usually call for wringing grated potatoes dry in a kitchen towel. This step removes excess moisture from the potatoes so they will become crisp when cooked, but it can be messy. Here's a neater way to dry grated potatoes.

Place the grated potatoes in a salad spinner and spin them dry. Remember that grated potatoes will discolor in just a few minutes, so work quickly.

Number 297

Potatoes | FOLDING HASH BROWNS

For us, the best hash browns have as much potato crunch as possible. Removing excess water from the grated potatoes before cooking will help them crisp up in the pan. This folding technique ensures that every bite is packed with crunch.

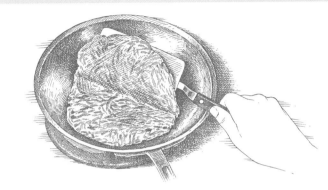

Once the hash brown has been browned on both sides, fold the cake over, omelet style. When cut into wedges, each piece will now have four crisp surfaces—two inside and two outside.

Number 298

Ravioli | IMPROMPTU WRAPPERS

Store-bought wonton wrappers can be used as a substitute for homemade pasta when making ravioli.

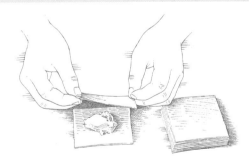

1. Lay one wrapper on a work surface. Place some homemade filling on top. Brush the edges of the wrapper with a little water and then cover with a second wrapper.

2. Use the tines of a fork to seal the edges of the ravioli shut. Make sure that the seal is tight so that the filling won't leak out while the ravioli are being cooked.

Number 299

Rhubarb | PEELING

Rhubarb stalks, especially thick ones, are covered with a stringy outside layer that should be removed before cooking. Make sure to cut away and discard the leaves, which are inedible.

1. Trim both ends of the stalk. Partially slice a thin disk from the bottom of the trimmed stalk, being careful not to cut all the way through. Gently pull the partially attached disk away from the stalk, pull back the outer peel, and discard.

2. Make a second cut partially through the bottom of the stalk in the reverse direction. Pull back the peel on the other side of the stalk and discard. The rhubarb is now ready to be sliced or chopped as needed in recipes.

Number 300

Rice | RINSING

Many recipes for rice pilaf start by rinsing the rice until the water runs clear—a process that can take as many as four or five rinses. Here's how to wash away excess starch without losing a single grain.

Place the rice in a large bowl, cover the bowl with a mesh splatter screen, and fill with water. When the bowl is full, simply hold the splatter screen tight against the bowl and pour off the water. The rice stays in the bowl and is ready to be rinsed again.

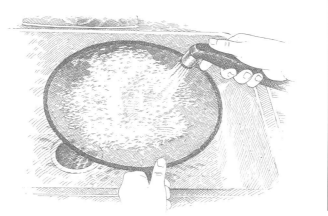

Number 301

Rice | STEAMING FOR FLUFFY TEXTURE

Whether cooking regular rice or making pilaf, we find that a dry, fluffy texture is best.

Once the rice is tender, remove the pan from the heat, place a clean kitchen towel folded in half over the saucepan, replace the lid, and set aside for 10 minutes. Residual heat continues to steam the rice and improves its texture, while the towel absorbs excess moisture that would otherwise condense on the lid and eventually fall back into the rice and make it mushy.

Number 302

Saffron | CRUMBLING TO RELEASE FLAVOR

Saffron threads are the world's most expensive spice, so you certainly want to extract every drop of flavor. Here's how to get the most bang for your buck.

Before adding saffron to a stew or soup, crumble the threads between your fingers to break up the saffron. Crumbling releases flavorful oils and helps the saffron dissolve in the liquid.

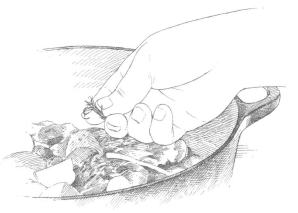

Number 303

Salad Spinners | GETTING BETTER LEVERAGE

Salad spinners with a top-mounted turn crank can rumble and vibrate during use. Here's how to make them a little smoother and easier to use.

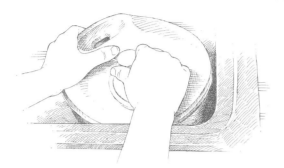

Place the salad spinner in the corner of your sink. This increases your leverage by lowering the height of the crank. This extra leverage also acts to push the spinner down to the sink floor and into the sink walls, thereby stabilizing the spinner.

Number 304

Salmon | REMOVING PINBONES

A salmon fillet will occasionally contain a few tiny white bones called pinbones. These bones are smaller and thinner than a toothpick and can be hard to find.

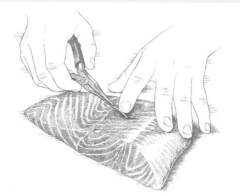

1. Before cooking, rub the tips of your fingers gently over the surface of each salmon fillet to locate any pinbones. They will feel like small bumps.

2. If you find any bones, use a clean pair of needle-nosed pliers or tweezers to pull the bones out.

Number 305

Salmon | TURNING A FILLET INTO STEAK

Many people prefer fillets to steaks because they would rather not deal with the bones. But because they are thinner at the edges, salmon fillets do not cook evenly. Some people may like the gradation from well-done at the edges to rare in the center, but others may not. Steaks have an even thickness and cook evenly from edge to edge. Here's a neat way to turn a fillet into a boneless steak.

1. Start by cutting lengthwise through a 3-inch-wide fillet down to, but not through, the skin.

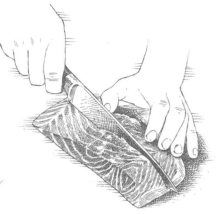

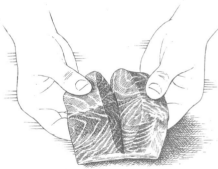

2. Fold the two flesh pieces out, with the skin acting as a hinge.

3. A 3-inch-wide fillet will now look like a steak, but without any bones, and have an even thickness of 1½ inches. The cooking time for mock steaks is the same as for regular fillets. The one drawback to this method is that the skin won't crisp, since it is sandwiched in the middle of the steak.

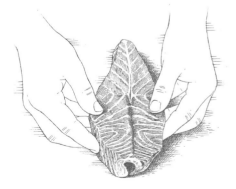

Number 306

Salt | KEEP IT SHAKABLE

Cooks who live in hot, humid climates know that salt often clumps in the shaker, making it difficult to sprinkle onto foods at the table.

Add a few grains of uncooked rice to the shaker. The rice will absorb excess moisture and keep the salt crystals from clumping together.

Number 307

Scallions | SLICING WITH SCISSORS

Slicing or chopping scallions with a knife often crushes their natural tube shape and spoils their appearance. Use this method with scallions as well as chives.

Starting at the green end, use scissors to cut neat, intact pieces of scallion.

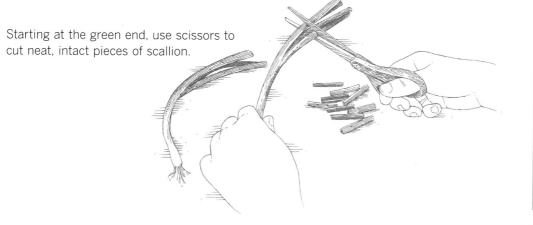

Number 308

Scallops | REMOVING TENDONS

The small, rough-textured, crescent-shaped muscle that attaches the scallop to the shell is often not removed during processing. It will toughen if heated and should be removed before cooking.

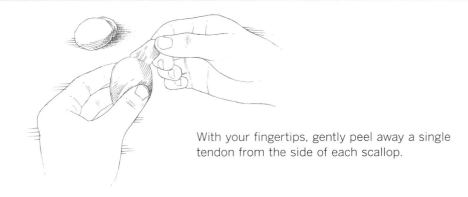

With your fingertips, gently peel away a single tendon from the side of each scallop.

Number 309

Shallots | MINCING

There are several ways to mince a shallot. We like this technique, which also works with garlic.

1. Place the peeled bulb flat-side down on a work surface and slice crosswise almost to (but not through) the root end.

2. Make a number of parallel cuts through the top of the shallot down to the work surface.

3. Finally, make very thin slices perpendicular to the lengthwise cuts made in step 2.

Number 310

Shortening | MESS-FREE MEASURING CUPS

Many pie bakers have experienced the frustration of trying to clean measuring cups that have contained a solid fat such as shortening or lard. Here's a good way to avoid the mess.

1. Line the measuring cup with plastic wrap before adding the fat.

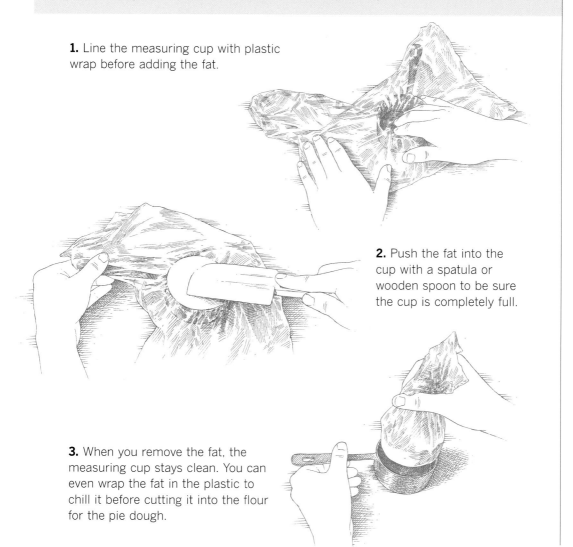

2. Push the fat into the cup with a spatula or wooden spoon to be sure the cup is completely full.

3. When you remove the fat, the measuring cup stays clean. You can even wrap the fat in the plastic to chill it before cutting it into the flour for the pie dough.

Number 311

Shrimp | DEVEINING WITH SHELLS ON

When cooked by dry heat (pan-searing or grilling), shrimp are best left in their shells. The shells hold in moisture, and also flavor the shrimp as they cook. However, eating shrimp cooked in their shells can be a challenge. Slitting the shells is a good compromise—it makes the shrimp easy to peel at the table, but the shrimp are still protected as they cook.

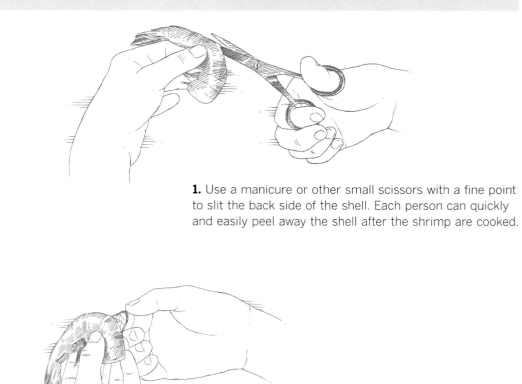

1. Use a manicure or other small scissors with a fine point to slit the back side of the shell. Each person can quickly and easily peel away the shell after the shrimp are cooked.

2. Slitting the back of the shell makes it easy to devein the shrimp as well. (Except when the vein is especially dark and thick, we leave it in, but you may choose otherwise.) As you slit the shells, you will cut into the meat a bit and expose the vein. Use the tip of the scissors to lift up the vein, and then grab it with your fingers and discard.

Number 312

Shrimp | GRILLING

Shrimp should be skewered before grilling to keep them from falling through the grate. However, every cook has been frustrated by shrimp that spin around on skewers and are impossible to turn.

 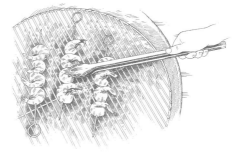

1. Thread the shrimp by passing the skewer through the body near the tail, folding the shrimp over, and passing the skewer through the shrimp again near the head.

2. Long-handled tongs make it easy to turn hot skewers on the grill. Lightly grab onto a single shrimp to turn the entire skewer.

Number 313

Shrimp | STRETCHING STEAMED SHRIMP

Sometimes large shrimp can be awkward to serve at a cocktail party. At other times, you may want to "stretch" the amount of shrimp available when unexpected guests drop by. Here's how to cut a single shrimp in two pieces that are easier to eat.

1. Peel the shrimp as usual, then halve them lengthwise and steam as usual.

2. The cooked shrimp will curl into spirals and make an attractive presentation.

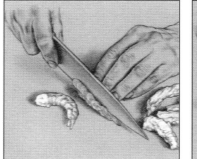 

Number 314

Soufflés | CREATING A FOIL COLLAR

To make soufflés rise high above the rim of the dish, we find it best to attach a foil collar to the side of the dish before filling it. As the soufflé bakes, the collar provides a surface against which it can rise. This technique works with chilled as well as baked soufflés.

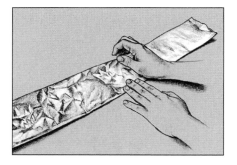

1. Cut a piece of foil 3 inches longer than the circumference of the soufflé dish and fold it lengthwise into fourths.

2. Wrap the foil strip around the upper half of the soufflé dish and secure the overlap with tape. Tape the collar to the outside of the soufflé dish.

3. Fill the soufflé dish and bake or chill as directed. Just before serving, carefully remove the collar.

Number 315

Soups | DRIP-FREE LADLING

Here's an easy way to keep drips and spills to a minimum when ladling soups or stews.

Before lifting the filled ladle up and out of the pot, dip the bottom back into the pot, so the liquid comes about halfway up the ladle. The tension on the surface of the soup grabs any drips and pulls them back into the pot.

Number 316

Soups | QUICK-CHILLING

Soups and stews often taste best the day after they are made. They should be cooled to room temperature before being refrigerated. However, if you cook in the evening, this can mean waiting up until the wee hours just to get the soup in the refrigerator. Here's a quick way to bring down the temperature of a hot pot of soup or stew.

Fill a large plastic beverage bottle almost to the top with water, seal it, and freeze it. Use the frozen bottle to stir the soup or stew in the pot; the ice inside the bottle will cool down the soup or stew rapidly without diluting it.

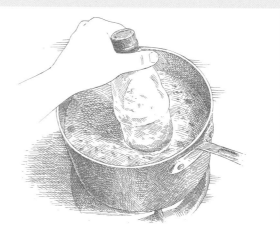

Number 317

Spaghetti | BREAKING LONG PASTA STRANDS NEATLY

Though we don't usually recommend breaking strands that we plan to sauce and eat, broken spaghetti or linguine is used in some casseroles, such as turkey Tetrazzini. Here's a neat way to break spaghetti strands in half without causing short shards of pasta to fly every which way in the kitchen.

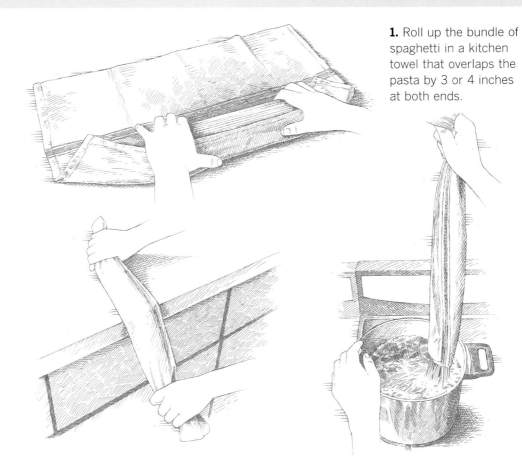

1. Roll up the bundle of spaghetti in a kitchen towel that overlaps the pasta by 3 or 4 inches at both ends.

2. Holding both ends firmly, center the rolled bundle over the edge of a table or counter. Push down with both hands to break the pasta in the middle of the bundle.

3. Holding the bundle vertically over the pot of boiling water, release the bottom of the cloth so that the pasta slides neatly into the pot.

Number 318

Spices | STORING EFFICIENTLY

It can be frustrating to sort through a sea of spice bottles, lifting and replacing each one, to find what you are looking for. Here's a better way to find spices and keep track of their age.

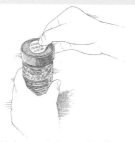 

1. Using stick-on dots, write the name and purchase date on top of spice jars when you get them home from the market.

2. It is easy to locate and extract the spice you want and to know when a spice is past its prime and should be replaced. Dry spices should be discarded after one year.

Number 319

Spices | MEASURING NEATLY

Measuring spices can be tricky, especially if measuring spoons won't fit into narrow bottles. Also, many cooks measure spices right over the mixing bowl, which can lead to overspicing of foods. Here's how we measure spices, leaveners, and salt in our test kitchen.

1. Working over a sheet of parchment paper, wax paper, or paper towel, fill the measuring spoon, mounding excess spice over the spoon. With a flat spatula, sweep off the excess onto the paper below.

2. Add the measured spice to the mixing bowl, then fold the paper in half and slide the excess spice back into the bottle.

Number 320

Spices | APPLYING SEASONINGS TO A ROAST

To ensure that meat is well seasoned, it's important to apply seasonings evenly. This is especially important when coating a roast with cracked peppercorns or a spice rub for grilling. Here's how we apply seasonings to beef tenderloin, pork loin, and other large roasts before cooking.

Set the roast on a sheet of plastic wrap and rub it all over with a little oil. Sprinkle with salt, pepper, or other spices, then lift the plastic wrap up and around the meat to press on the excess.

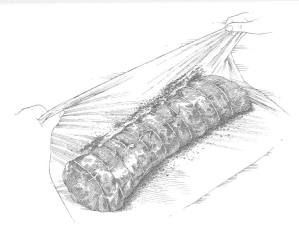

Number 321

Spices | TO REMOVE SPICES EASILY

Some soup or sauce recipes call for cooking spices and herbs in the liquid and then removing them before serving. Instead of fishing around for black peppercorns, cloves, star anise, bay leaves, or garlic, try this tip.

Place the spices in a mesh tea ball and then drop the closed ball into the pot. Hang the chain over the side of the pot for easy removal.

Number 322

Squash | CUTTING WITH A CLEAVER AND MALLET

Winter squash are notoriously difficult to cut. Even the best chef's knives can struggle with their thick skins and odd shapes. We prefer to use a cleaver and mallet when working with large winter squash.

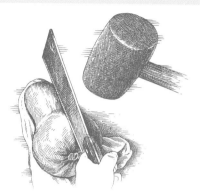 

1. Set the squash on a damp kitchen towel to hold it in place. Position the cleaver on the skin of the squash.

2. Strike the back of the cleaver with a mallet to drive the cleaver deep into the squash. Continue to hit the cleaver with the mallet until the cleaver cuts through the squash and opens it up.

Number 323

Squash | REMOVING SEEDS IN ONE SWOOP

Digging through the seed cavity of a winter squash to remove seeds and strings can be tedious, even with a large spoon. Here's a better way to ready squash for cooking.

Use an ice cream scoop shaped like a cupped hand to cut out all the seeds and strings without damaging the flesh. Because the edge on this kind of scoop is very sharp, it cuts easily, and because the scoop is larger than a spoon, it can remove more seeds in a single swipe.

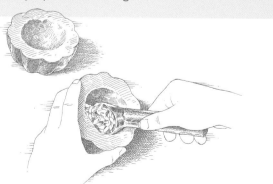

Number 324

Steaming | PREVENTING SCORCHED PANS

Sometimes a cook can become distracted and forget a pan of simmering water on the stove. When using just a little bit of water and a steamer basket, the pot can run dry. Eventually, the heat will ruin the pot and can cause a dangerous situation. When steaming foods that take a long time to cook, such as artichokes, here's a neat way to figure out when the pot needs more water.

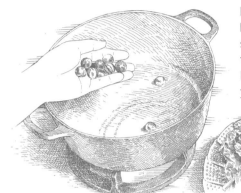

Before cooking, place a few glass marbles in the bottom of the pan. Add the water and the steamer basket, cover, and cook as usual. When the water level drops too low, the marbles will begin to rattle around and the racket will remind you to add more water.

Number 325

Steaming | TURNING YOUR WOK INTO A STEAMER

Because of its wide shape and domed lid, a wok is the perfect vessel for steaming. However, you need a flat platform on which to place foods. This method is especially good for steaming fish.

1. Set four sturdy chopsticks, two running lengthwise and two running crosswise, in a wok.

2. Place the food to be steamed in a glass pie plate. Set the pie plate on the platform created by the chopsticks, add water, cover the wok, and steam.

Number 326

Stews | CUTTING YOUR OWN CUBES

Packages of "stew meat" sold in supermarkets often contain misshapen scraps of varying sizes. For even cooking, pieces should be 1½-inch cubes. In addition, the meat can come from different parts of the animal.

Instead of buying stew meat, buy a boneless roast (from the chuck for beef stew) and cut it into chunks yourself. This way you can also trim excess bits of fat and gristle.

Number 327

Stews | DEFATTING WITH A LETTUCE LEAF

It's easy enough to remove excess fat from a brothy soup in a flash—use a gravy separator. With a chunky stew, this method just won't work.

Instead, place a large lettuce leaf on the surface of the stew; it will absorb excess fat, and then you can remove and discard the leaf.

Number 328

Stir-Frying | JUDGING HEAT LEVEL IN THE PAN

We find that a large nonstick skillet works better than a wok when stir-frying on an American stove. The flat bottom of the skillet matches better with conventional burners, and the pan gets hot all over. A wok is designed to rest in a conical pit where flames can heat all sides. On a stove, only the bottom of a wok really gets hot. Besides the right pan, stir-frying demands a lot of heat.

When the ingredients are ready, set the skillet over high heat for several minutes. To see if the pan is hot enough, hold your hand an inch above the pan. When the pan is so hot you can keep your hand there for only three seconds, add the oil, heat it briefly, and then start cooking.

Number 329

Stir-Frying | ADDING GARLIC AND GINGER

One of the biggest complaints home cooks have about stir-fries is that the garlic and ginger can burn and give the food a burnt, harsh flavor. Instead of adding the garlic and ginger at the start of the cooking process, try this method.

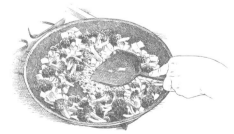

1. Stir-fry the meat, seafood, or poultry and remove it from the pan. Stir-fry the vegetables. Once the vegetables are crisp-tender, clear the center of the pan, add the garlic, ginger, scallions, chiles, or other aromatics, and drizzle with a little oil.

2. Use a wok shovel/spatula to mash the garlic and ginger as they cook. After about 10 seconds, stir the garlic and ginger mixture back into the vegetables, add the seared meat, seafood, or poultry along with the sauce, and finish cooking.

Number 330

Stocks | STRAINING OUT SOLIDS

Once you have simmered chicken backs or fish heads to make stock, it can be cumbersome to strain out the solids. The solids can splash, and you end up losing a fair amount of liquid in the process.

We use a large pot with a pasta insert to make stock. When the solids have given up their flavor, simply lift the insert and its cargo out of the pot easily and neatly. For clarity, the remaining liquid should be strained, but without any large solids in the pot this job is much easier and neater.

Number 331

Stocks | FREEZING IN CONVENIENT PORTIONS

Many recipes call for small amounts of stock. Instead of defrosting a large container of homemade stock just to get a cup or two, you can freeze stock in small portions. If you don't have an oversized muffin tin with a nonstick coating, try tip 332 on page 210.

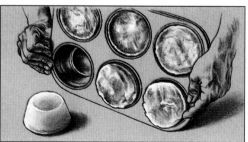

1. Ladle the stock into oversized, nonstick muffin tins, each of which holds just under one cup of stock, and freeze.

2. When the stock is frozen, twist the muffin tin in the same manner you twist an ice tray, tapping the bottom with a knife to loosen the frozen stock if necessary. Place the blocks of frozen stock in a plastic bag, seal tightly, and use, one at a time, as needed.

Number 332

Stocks | FREEZING IN PLASTIC POUCHES

Here's another good way to freeze stock in small portions. Stock frozen this way takes up very little room in the freezer.

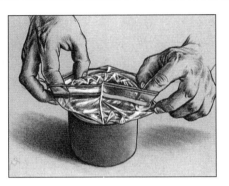

1. Line a coffee mug with a quart-sized zipper-lock plastic bag. (This keeps the bag open so both hands will be free for pouring.)

2. Fill the bag almost to the top with room temperature stock and seal it. Repeat until all the stock has been placed in bags.

3. Stack the bags flat in a large, shallow roasting pan and freeze. Once the stock is solidly frozen, the bags can be removed from the pan and stored in the freezer wherever there's room.

Number 333

Strawberries | STORING

Moisture and air are the enemies of fresh berries and will hasten their decline. We find this method keeps strawberries fresh for at least several days.

Place unwashed berries in an airtight container, separating the layers of berries with sheets of paper towel, which will absorb excess moisture and slow down the softening process.

Number 334

Strawberries | HULLING

Early-season strawberries can have tough, white cores that are best removed. If you don't own a strawberry huller, you can improvise with a plastic drinking straw.

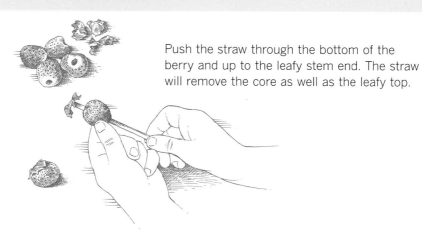

Push the straw through the bottom of the berry and up to the leafy stem end. The straw will remove the core as well as the leafy top.

Number 335

Stuffing | TAKING THE TEMPERATURE

When cooking a stuffed chicken or turkey, it's important to measure the temperature of the stuffing as well as the bird. Stuffing is fully cooked and safe to eat at 165 degrees.

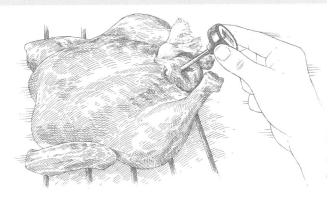

Insert an instant-read thermometer into the center of the cavity to measure the internal temperature of the stuffing.

Number 336

Tartlets | FILLING INDIVIDUAL SHELLS

Filling individual shells with a custard or other filling can be both messy and tedious. To fill the shells with speed and precision, use a bulb baster.

1. Place the filling in a measuring cup, then fill the bulb baster from the cup.

2. Move the bulb baster directly over the tartlet shell and squirt out just the right amount of filling. Repeat until all the shells are filled.

Number 337

Tarts | ROLLING THE DOUGH

Sweet tart pastry, called pâte sucrée, can be sticky. The same can be true of regular pie dough. Instead of coating the work surface with a thick layer of flour (which will just make the dough dry and crumbly), use this method for rolling out sticky dough.

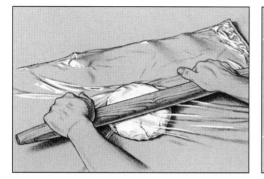

1. Place the chilled dough round between two sheets of plastic wrap. Roll the dough outward from the center with even pressure.

2. When the dough has reached the desired size, peel off the top sheet of plastic, flip the dough into the tart pan, then peel off the second sheet of plastic.

Number 338

Tarts | LEVELING THE EDGES

The edges of a tart shell should be flush with the rim on the pan. Here's how to remove excess dough.

Once the dough has been fitted into the tart pan, run the rolling pin over the top of the pan to break off any dough that rises above the rim.

213

Number 339

Tarts | STORING AN UNBAKED SHELL

Tart dough that has been rolled out and fitted into a tart pan can be refrigerated for a day or two or frozen for several months. Here's how we protect the delicate pastry from picking up off flavors or falling victim to freezer burn.

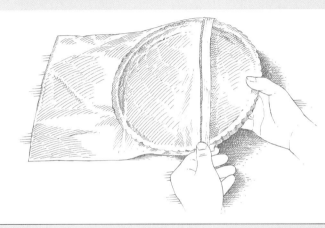

An 8- or 9-inch unbaked tart shell can be slipped right into a gallon-sized zipper-lock plastic bag. Seal the bag and then refrigerate or freeze as desired.

Number 340

Tarts | PROTECTING THE EDGE FROM BURNING

Sometimes the edges of a tart shell can burn before the bottom is cooked through and nicely browned. Instead of covering the edges of the tart shell with aluminum foil, here's a simple way to protect the crust.

If you notice that the edges are browning too quickly, invert the ring from a second, larger tart pan, place it over the endangered crust, and continue baking.

Number 341

Tarts | EASY UNMOLDING

Once a tart has baked and cooled, you need to remove the outer ring in order to serve the tart. Some cooks try to lift the removable pan bottom up with their hand, but this causes the ring to slide down your arm like a hula hoop. Here's an easy way to remove the ring, without any complicated gymnastic maneuvers.

Set a wide, stout can, such as a 28-ounce tomato can, on a flat surface. Set the cooled tart and pan on top of the can. Hold the pan ring and gently pull it downward—the can will support the pan base with the tart as you remove the ring. Once the ring reaches the work surface, transfer the tart and pan bottom to a serving platter.

Number 342

Tarts | IMPROVISED COVER

A footed cake plate is probably the safest and most attractive place to hold a baked tart. But what about the leftovers? A cake stand won't fit in most refrigerators.

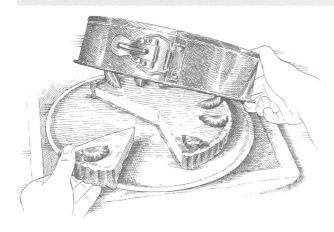

Place the tart, which will still be on the removable pan bottom, in the refrigerator. Invert a springform pan and place it over the tart. The tart will be protected and you can even stack other items on top of the sturdy and level springform pan.

215

Number 343

Tea|REMOVING TEA BAGS

A pitcher of iced tea requires the use of several tea bags. To keep the tea from tasting bitter, the bags should be removed after steeping for three minutes. Here's an easy way to remove the tea bags without having to reach into the hot liquid.

1. Tie the tea bag strings together, then slide a bamboo skewer or single chopstick through the knot before tightening it.

2. Position the skewer across the top of the pan with the tea bags immersed in the water. When the tea is finished brewing, lift the skewer up and away and you'll take the spent tea bags right with it.

Number 344

Tomato Paste|PORTIONING OUT PASTE

Recipes often call for just a tablespoon or two of tomato paste. Unfortunately, the rest of the can often ends up turning brown in the refrigerator and then being discarded. Here's a better way to save excess tomato paste.

1. Open both ends of the can. Remove the lid from one end and use the lid at the other end to push the paste out onto a sheet of plastic wrap.

2. Wrap plastic around the tomato paste and freeze until solid.

3. When you need tomato paste, cut off only as much as you need for a particular recipe, then rewrap the frozen log and return it to the freezer.

Number 345

Tomatoes | CORING

Tomatoes are almost always cored—that is, the tough stem is removed and discarded. Before chopping or slicing a tomato, we always core it. We also suggest coring before peeling, since coring provides a practical point of departure when it's time to peel.

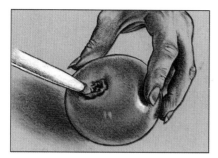

Place the tomato on its side on a work surface. Holding the tomato stable with one hand, insert the tip of a paring knife about 1 inch into the tomato at an angle just outside the core. Move the paring knife with a sawing motion, at the same time rotating the tomato toward you until the core is cut free.

Number 346

Tomatoes | SLICING

Unless you have a very sharp knife, tomato skin can resist the knife edge and the tomato becomes crushed. Here's a neat trick that starts with a cored tomato.

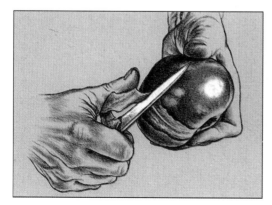

1. Use a paring knife to remove a strip of skin from the exposed core area down to the blossom end of the tomato.

2. Slice the tomato along the skinned strip so that the knife does not have to cut through skin before it can enter the tomato.

217

Tomatoes | PEELING

There are many recipes that call for peeling fresh tomatoes. If left on, the peels can separate from the flesh and roll up into hard, unappetizing bits when the tomatoes are cooked. Here's how to get rid of the skins on standard round tomatoes as well as on oblong plum, or Roma, tomatoes.

1. Place cored tomatoes in boiling water, no more than five at a time. Boil until skins split and begin to curl around the cored area of the tomato, about 15 seconds for very ripe tomatoes or up to 30 seconds for firmer, underripe ones. Remove the tomatoes from the water with a slotted spoon or mesh skimmer and place them in a bowl of ice water to stop the cooking process and cool the tomatoes.

2. With a paring knife, peel the skins away using the curled edges at the core as your point of departure. (The bowl of ice water fulfills a helpful second function—the skins will slide right off the blade of the knife if you dip the blade into the water.)

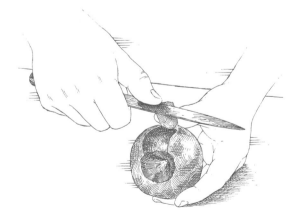

Number 348

Tomatoes | SEEDING

The seeds are watery and sometimes bitter and are often removed before chopping a tomato. These techniques work for both peeled and unpeeled tomatoes. Note that because of their different shapes, round and plum (also called Roma) tomatoes are seeded differently.

 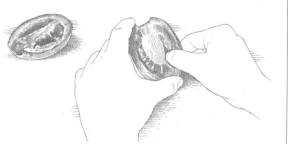

A. To seed a round tomato, halve the cored tomato along the equator. If the tomato is ripe and juicy, gently give it a squeeze and shake out the seeds and gelatinous material. If not, scoop them out with your finger or a small spoon.

B. To seed an oblong plum tomato, halve the cored tomato lengthwise, cutting through the core end. Cut through the inner membrane with a paring knife or break through it with your finger and scoop out the seeds and gelatinous material.

Number 349

Tongs | STORING SAFELY

We love spring-loaded tongs for turning foods in skillets and out on the grill. But put those tongs in a small drawer with other tools, and they can cause chaos. The tongs can become tangled with other tools and can even prevent the drawer from opening. Here's a safe way to store spring-loaded tongs.

Slide the closed tongs into a heavy-duty cardboard tube from a roll of plastic wrap. The tongs can then be stored in the drawer without opening or interfering with other tools.

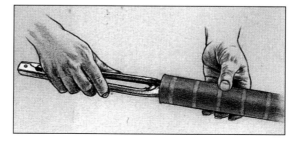

Number 350

Tortillas | BULK STORAGE

The tortillas sold in bulk packages at warehouse-type supermarkets are much less expensive than the smaller packages sold at the grocery store. But if you freeze the whole package, you'll end up ripping many tortillas as you try to free just a couple from the frozen block.

Before freezing, separate the tortillas with sheets of wax or parchment paper. Place the stack of separated tortillas in freezer bags and freeze as usual. The paper dividers make it easy to pull individual tortillas from the frozen pile.

Number 351

Turkey | BRINING OUT OF THE REFRIGERATOR

For years, we've advocated soaking a turkey in a saltwater bath before roasting. This process, called brining, produces a moist, well-seasoned bird. The problem is where to keep the turkey as it brines. A large stock pot or clean bucket large enough to hold a turkey, two gallons of cold water, and salt simply won't fit in most refrigerators. A cool basement or garage can be used. When those options are not available, try this method.

Line a large stock pot or clean bucket with a turkey-sized oven bag. Place several large, clean frozen ice gel packs in the brine with the turkey. Tie the bag shut, cover the container, and place in a cool spot for 4 hours. Because of the short brining time, you must use a lot of salt—either two cups of table salt or four cups of kosher salt. Once the turkey is brined, remember to rinse the bird well under running water and pat dry with paper towels.

Number 352

Turkey | REMOVING PART OF THE WINGS

Large turkeys can hang over the side of even the largest roasting pan and drip fat onto the oven floor. Here's how to keep your kitchen smoke-free and get some extra parts to make gravy.

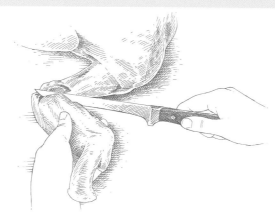

Remove the first two joints of the wing, leaving only the drumette attached to the bird. Reserve the wings for use along with the neck, tail, and giblets when making gravy.

Number 353

Turkey | TRUSSING THE CAVITY SHUT

Once the bird has been stuffed, you must close the cavity to prevent the stuffing from spilling out.

Cut wooden skewers into four pieces, each about 5 inches long. Push the skewers through the skin on either side of the cavity. Use a 20-inch piece of heavy kitchen twine to lace the cavity shut, as if lacing a pair of boots.

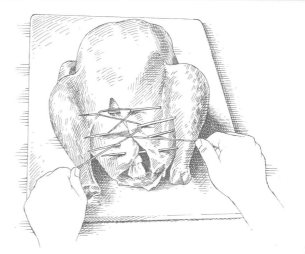

Number 354

Turkey | KNOWING WHEN IT'S DONE

For many cooks, the hardest part of preparing Thanksgiving dinner is figuring out when to take the turkey out of the oven. Use an instant-read thermometer properly, and you will never overcook a turkey again.

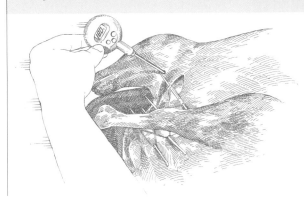

The breast tastes fine when cooked to an internal temperature of 160 degrees. However, the thighs are not really done until they reach an internal temperature of 175 to 180 degrees. For this reason, take the internal temperature of the bird in the thickest part of the thigh, as shown. You should also check the stuffing (see tip 335 on page 212); it should register 165 degrees.

Number 355

Turkey | LEVERAGED LIFTING

Transferring a hot turkey from the roasting rack onto the carving board can be a messy, precarious maneuver. We find that two long-handled wooden spoons make this job easier.

Insert the bowl ends of the spoons into either end of the bird's cavity so that the handles stick out. Grasp the handles, really choking up on them so your hands are right next to the turkey, and lift the bird off the rack (which you may have to hold in place with the help of a passerby in the kitchen).

Number 356

Twine | KEEPING IT CLEAN

When tying meat, you want to keep the ball of butcher's twine away from the raw food.

Place the twine on the handle of a meat pounder to prevent contamination of the entire spool.

Number 357

Twine | LEARNING THE ROPES

Many cooks have trouble tying roasts properly. Here's a clean way to practice your knotting skills.

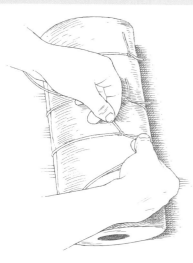

Tie strands of butcher's twine around a roll of paper towels. Once your have mastered the art of knotting, it's time to move on to food.

Number 358

V-Rack | SECURING TO ROASTING PAN

If your V-rack and your roasting pan are not well matched in size, or if you have a nonstick roasting pan, the V-rack and its heavy contents can slide around the pan and create a dangerous situation. Here's how to stabilize a slippery rack.

Make four ropes of twisted aluminum foil and twist two onto each end of the V-rack base to fasten. Feed the free ends of the ropes through the pan handles and twist to fasten them around the handles.

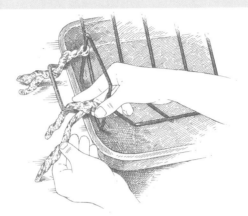

Number 359

V-Rack | STABILIZING ON THE GRILL

A turkey roasted on the grill can be delicious. But even if the coals are banked to one side of the grill, the skin can burn if the turkey is cooked right on the grate. We prefer to elevate the bird in a V-rack. However, the base of some V-racks may slip through the bars on your grill grate.

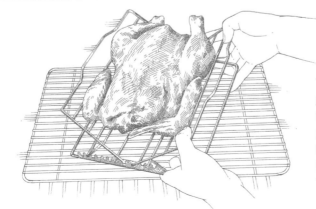

To steady the V-rack, cover the grill grate with a wire cooling rack for baking so that its bars run perpendicular to the bars on the grill grate. The cooling rack provides a stable surface on which the base of the V-rack can rest.

Number 360

Vanilla | REMOVING SEEDS FROM A BEAN

A vanilla bean adds the truest flavor to ice cream, custards, and puddings. The seeds inside the bean have the most flavor. Here's how to free the seeds from the pod.

1. Use a small, sharp knife to cut the vanilla bean in half lengthwise.

2. Place the knife at one end of one bean half and press down to flatten the bean as you move the knife away from you and catch the seeds on the edge of the blade. Add the seeds as well as the pods to the liquid ingredients.

Number 361

Vegetable Peeler | SHARPENING

A paring knife can be used to restore the edge on a dulled peeler.

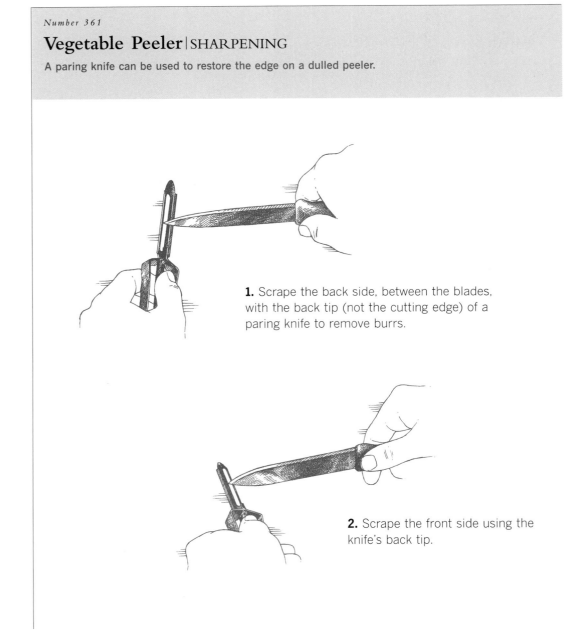

1. Scrape the back side, between the blades, with the back tip (not the cutting edge) of a paring knife to remove burrs.

2. Scrape the front side using the knife's back tip.

Number 362

Walnuts | SKINNING

The skins from toasted walnuts can impart a bitter taste to dishes. Here's a simple way to remove these thin skins.

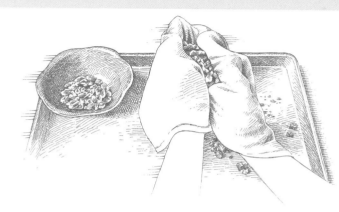

Once the nuts have been toasted, rub them inside a clean kitchen towel. The skins will separate from the nut meats.

Number 363

Wine Glasses | DRYING ON CHOPSTICKS

With one wrong move or an inadvertent bump, a dish rack filled with drying dishes can wreak havoc on delicate stemware. Here's a good way to dry glasses in a safe corner of the counter, out of harm's way.

Set up chopsticks (the square-sided kind are best) parallel to each other and about 1¹/₂ to 2 inches apart on the counter. Place the wet wineglasses on the chopsticks to dry. The slight elevation off the counter allows air to circulate into the glasses and speeds drying.

Number 364

Zucchini | GRATING

Many recipes call for salting zucchini before cooking to rid this vegetable of excess water. Drier zucchini browns better and tastes better. However, there's not always time to salt zucchini and wait for an hour or two. Here's a quick way to remove excess water. This technique also works with yellow summer squash.

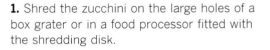

1. Shred the zucchini on the large holes of a box grater or in a food processor fitted with the shredding disk.

2. Wrap the shredded zucchini in paper towels and squeeze out as much liquid as possible. When dry, the zucchini is ready to be sautéed.

Number 365

Zucchini | SEEDING

When making stuffed zucchini, it is necessary to scoop out the seeds with a spoon. In fresh zucchini, the seeds and flesh can be very firm, making this job difficult. Here's a neat way to loosen up the seeds. This tip also works with eggplant.

1. Place the zucchini on a work surface and roll with slight pressure being applied by your hands. The pressure will soften the insides and loosen the seeds.

2. Halve the rolled zucchini lengthwise and scoop out the seeds with a spoon.

Index